HOLY GHOSTED

AUTUMN MILES

CHARISMA HOUSE

Cataloging-in-Publication Data is on file with the Library of Congress.
International Standard Book Number: 978-1-63641-543-7
E-book ISBN: 978-1-63641-544-4

1 2025
Printed in the United States of America

Most Charisma Media products are available at special quantity discounts for bulk purchase for sales promotions, premiums, fund-raising, and educational needs. For details, call us at (407) 333-0600 or visit our website at charismamedia.com.

CONTENTS

Be of sober spirit, be on the alert. Your adversary, the devil, prowls around like a roaring lion, seeking someone to devour. But resist him, firm in your faith, knowing that the same experiences of suffering are being accomplished by your brethren who are in the world. After you have suffered for a little while, the God of all grace, who called you to His eternal glory in Christ, will Himself perfect, confirm, strengthen and establish you. To Him be dominion forever and ever. Amen.

—1 Peter 5:8–11, emphasis added

Chapter 1
HOLY GHOSTED

Truly You are a God who hides Yourself,
O God of Israel, the Savior.
—Isaiah 45:15, MEV

S HE IS PLAYING right into our hand. We almost have her. She's almost ours. Keep the thoughts coming. Increase the thoughts of death and abuse. Put on maximum pressure. Don't let up. It's time to double down," one demon shrieked to another as he relayed the information.

"I can see her cracking. Her body language alone is telling us that she is almost ready," the other demon replied.

"Her life is too valuable to YHWH. We have to stop this one. We have to keep applying pressure," the first demon answered.

"She's close. Do you see her breathing heavy? She is right there. Her heart rate is spiking. Ha, she played right into our hands. She was an easy target," the second demon replied.

"This will be a great victory for us and the master," the first demon answered.

"She's fidgeting. She's tossing in her bed. I think she's ready; it's time to start telling her how she should end her life. Give her ideas and options. She's never thought like this before. She won't know what to do. Tell her that her life is too much for her to handle, and the pressure that she's living in is too great to overcome. But confuse her. Tell her she needs to die, and she should, but remind her that she doesn't want to. We don't want to be too obvious."

"Did you see that? Her eyes popped open. It's working. She's considering it. Tell her she doesn't have any choice but death. Remind her that God is silent so He must not care about her—He let all this happen to her. Steady. Steady. We don't want to lose this one. She'll be a problem for us if we let her go," the first demon said.

"Let's just wait it out. We are patient. Let's just let these thoughts ruminate for a second. Let her mind receive our lies. Oh, they are so effective. I love it when these types are out of options and weak. They forget God. Ha. They turn their backs on Him so easily. She will take the bait; these types always do. Remember what the master said, 'Patience is our greatest ally,'" the second demon remembered.

"OK, I'll stand by. I don't want to pause for too long. The Holy Spirit may come and disrupt our plan. We've been working on this girl for too long to mess it up now," the first demon agreed.

"Well, the Holy Spirit has been silent for years, but just in case, let's wrap this up tonight," the second demon replied.

"If the Light gets involved, it's game over for us," the first demon said.

"Wait, what's going on? Her breathing is slowing, and her heart rate is normalizing. What is happening? I'm using every trick I have permission to exercise. We are losing her," the second demon said.

"The Light just showed up. He was silent for so long. Why would He speak now?" the first demon replied.

"Because she is His. We just lost. Our best effort just failed. It wasn't strong enough to compete with the Light."

The spiritual tug-of-war wasn't just imagined; it was felt—felt in my breath, in my pulse, in the atmosphere.

I lay completely still in my dark bedroom, silent. My only company was the light spilling from the bathroom. Everything around me was still, but inside I was unraveling. The room was completely still except for the pounding of my heart and my heavy breathing. While all seemed silent, I could feel a war happening over me. Something—or someone—dark wanted me. I could feel it. It was palpable. There was an evil heaviness in the room. Darkness wasn't just the shadows in the bedroom; it was the sensation of the atmosphere. This presence wasn't new. This darkness had been around for years; it followed me. I had gotten used to it.

While this presence terrorized me most days, the consistency of it was something I had been able to manage. I didn't know how to get rid of it. In fact, I had stopped trying. For some time I had let it claim more ground in my life. Since God was silent, I had given this particular evil a voice in my head.

It brought a barrage of doubts and accusations:

- "Why is God silent?"

- "God hates you."

- "God isn't who He says He is."

- "You have no hope."

- "If God was truly who He says He is, why hasn't He delivered you from this relationship?"

THE WEIGHT OF DARKNESS

I grew accustomed to these thoughts. I had begun to believe almost all of them as truth. On this night, however, the thoughts and the darkness felt heavier than ever before. I couldn't shake it. The reality that my life was over at age twenty-one was hard to swallow. But there I was—done. I didn't know what was happening to my mind. I felt attacked. The barrage of thoughts came one right after the other, and I began a hard, fast downward spiral.

The thoughts were stronger than I was. I couldn't refute them. They were taking over my mind.

Evil was loud and aggressive, and hope was silent. Evil wanted me. Evil wanted what I could offer the world, so dark forces warred for my soul. I couldn't hear the battle, but I could feel the struggle. Feeling it was more real than anything else. The chaos was loud in and around me. Hope was silent. I hadn't heard from hope in so long that I had given up.

I could feel myself giving in to the weight of the darkness. Soon, evil would consume me, and I would surrender completely to it. I would give the darkness all the faith in God I had left because its power was too much for me.

THE LIGHT BREAKS THROUGH

As I lay silent and still, with only a racing heart, I could feel the dark energy shift in my bedroom. Something unfamiliar—something I didn't recognize, someone I had never heard from before—spoke to me and said, softly yet authoritatively, "Do you remember Me?"

While I had never directly heard from this person, I knew exactly who He was. He was the Lord, YHWH. I knew He was referring to Himself. He was the God I had learned about during my childhood; the One that, in recent years, I had secretly forsaken.

I knew of Him but had yet to meet Him. In that moment the Holy Spirit broke His silence—mere moments before Satan and the hordes of hell claimed victory over me.

God interrupted their conversation. He foiled their lengthy mission that had neared completion. And He stepped in and offered the one thing I was desperate for: hope.

When the Holy Spirit broke His silence to ransom me, He didn't judge me. He didn't condemn me. He asked me a question, "Do you remember Me?"

This question played on repeat in my spirit for several minutes. Desperately processing what this could mean—and knowing exactly who He was—I stayed still, not knowing how to reply. My heart rate began normalizing, and I caught myself, for the first time in several years, taking a deep breath.

While the Holy Spirit repeated the question, the thoughts of suicide and death began to lessen and eventually stopped. Now I could hear only one single question: "Do you remember Me?"

Looking back, that was all I needed to hear.

When God broke His silence and spoke to me, not only did He silence the enemy, but He also silenced the questions I had asked for years and used as a shield to keep Him out of my life.

That one question was so powerful that it enticed me to get out of my bed, walk to the next room, and for the first time ever, surrender my life to Him.

The Holy Spirit's word that night was more potent, more commanding, and more authoritative than years of the enemy's detailed plot, whose strategy was to get me to pledge allegiance and surrender my faith to Satan.

While I didn't hear the conversation above audibly, I

know this one truth: Evil was conversing on my behalf that night, and I have long imagined it sounded something like this. But heaven broke its silence and rendered evil defeated.

Hell had no claim on me.

WHY HOLY GHOSTED?

This story is not just my story. It's yours too. It's for those times when you can't hear God and you desperately need Him.

I wrote this book, *Holy Ghosted*, because it's time to remove any faux assumption that you are the only one who can't hear from God. Silent seasons are hard seasons. Holy silence is hard silence. Period.

Pastors, ministers, mature believers, new believers, and anyone in between all have the same need: hearing the voice of God to direct or comfort them.

When our lives are falling apart or we're struggling with a huge decision and God is silent—we all struggle. The most holy of holy people struggle. The most righteous of righteous people struggle.

What about the person who has been in ministry for a gazillion years, walking through the hardest season in their life and still can't find God's voice? They're struggling too.

This is one reason false prophets are on the rise.

Our spirit grasps at some hope that *their* prophecy over us might be true. We cling to their every word.

We can't hear from God, so we hope someone else can hear for us. We look to and follow them because our soul is starving for even the smallest glimpse of hope.

This is why celebrity pastors have been deified.

When God silences Himself, we hang on to the words of man in an intense effort for hope, and we begin to believe they can hear from God better than we can. This is why we write down and obsess over someone having a "word" for us—even when it doesn't align with our spirit. It's all a desperate attempt to hear from the Creator of heaven and earth—Jehovah.

Because, after all, that's what we want the most: to hear from God.

His comfort is what our soul aches for.

This book was born from that ache—from that sense of desperation to hear the voice of God through all the noise. I wrote this book in response to the number one question that my ministry has received over the past fifteen years.

In many different variations, we have been asked these questions countless times:

- "What do I do when God is silent?"

- "I can't hear from God, and I need direction. Please help me."

- "How do you hear from God? I don't know how. I need His help."

It's not just baby Christians asking; these are seasoned believers—even people in ministry—who are too embarrassed to admit they are struggling with God's silence. They see us as a neutral place and trust that we won't judge them for their honest admissions. I don't want anyone to feel "less than" for being in a silent season. That feeling—that something is wrong with you for not hearing God—is a trap from the enemy.

I'm weary of the lack of transparency in admitting we all struggle or have struggled with this silence. I know I have, and I believe we need to talk about it in a *relatable* way. Let's be real. David, in the Psalms, talks about his insatiable appetite to hear directly from God. He even begs God not to be silent, especially when he was going through the worst days of his life:

> How long, O LORD? Will you forget me forever? How long will you hide your face from me? How long must I take counsel in my soul and have sorrow in my heart all the day? How long shall my enemy be exalted over me? Consider and answer me, O LORD my God.
>
> —PSALM 13:1–3, ESV

So if David—the dude after God's own heart—begged God to answer him, I hypothesize that you have struggled too. If going through a silent season with God makes you less spiritual, then David would also be on your team.

WHAT SHOULD YOUR RELATIONSHIP WITH GOD SOUND LIKE?

We have been told and taught what the Christian is supposed to look like—how to act, how to behave, how to appear.

There is a common theme in Christian living that, in some way, we all seem to acknowledge. Whether it be from the patriarchs or matriarchs in Scripture or a mentor in your life who models godly living, we have an idea of what we think the Christian life should look like.

But what is less common—and far more important— is this question: What should your relationship with God *sound* like?

We are rarely told what is acceptable or even *preferable* when it comes to the sound of our relationship with God.

When God is silent in the most atrocious seasons of our lives, what does our relationship with Him sound like? What is appropriate? What is proper and acceptable? We don't want to disrespect Him, but where's the line we can't cross? Is there even a line?

Here's some real talk: Your relationship with God has a sound. What is it? Is it raw and unfiltered, or is it quiet and hesitant? Do you suppress what you truly want to say to the Lord because you don't want to make Him mad? Or do you speak openly and freely about how you feel? What is acceptable before the Lord? I'm glad you asked. (Ha!)

God's silence tends to bring out all sorts of things—beliefs, questions, and assumptions—we've kept buried. God's silence unleashes mindsets we dare not voice until we are at our wit's end, and even then we might not. Here's the kicker: God's silence is actually a form of communication.

Some would say it's the most powerful form. Why? Because lack of speaking has a way of getting us to a place where we understand ourselves more. When God is silent, we realize our faith may not be as robust and vigorous as we claim. When He's silent, we are called to question things He wants us to process. The questions get loud. Sometimes the point of His silence is to give us space for those questions to rise, so when He does speak, He can address them in His wisdom and truth—not our assumptions about Him.

THE SOUND OF DESPERATION

I want to normalize the sound of desperation for the Lord. It is biblical. And the sound of my relationship with the Lord since the night chronicled earlier? It's been desperation. This book will show you the often undiscussed side of what an unfiltered walk with God sounds like. The sound of your relationship with God is much more valuable than the look of it. Looks can be fake, but the sounds made in the secret place with the Lord allow you to measure your authenticity and intimacy.

Please forgive my raw vulnerability, but I have found that the only way to inspire authentic interchange with the Lord is to show the unedited version of my own walk.

Therefore, I'll be the willing illustration—me and my buddy Job.

My desire is for this book to be a resource and guide for anyone struggling to weather a silent season from God. My bestie Job and I will do our best, along with the unmatched Word of the Holy Spirit, to help you navigate the confusing and often faith-surrendering times when it feels like you've been *Holy Ghosted*, or when God is silent.

You don't have to give up on God.

You don't have to be bitter.

You don't have to be impatient.

God will speak.

You don't have to get mad—you simply need a plan, an awareness of what God may be doing, and how to persevere.

I've done it.

Job did it.

David did it.

You will master it too!

JOB: THE BOOK NO ONE WANTS TO PREACH ABOUT

The Book of Job—tucked right before the soul-soothing Psalms—is one that teachers, preachers, and believers widely ignore. Why? Because it's terrifying and tough to understand. Job loses everything at once, and God doesn't say a single word about it until the end. That doesn't exactly preach well.

It won't grow churches.

It won't inspire parishioners to give tithes.

It scares people.

So your girl is going there.

I studied it for you.

I highly suggest diving into the Book of Job like a triple-scooped, hot fudge sundae after your forty-day Daniel fast, but for now I've done my digging—and I have a treasure chest of wisdom to impart.

Trust me, I have studied multiple biblical scholars who have written extensively on Job. These biblical scholars wrote the books taught in seminaries around the world. My eyes hurt from the number of biblical commentaries I have consulted. They are many.

I have sought wise counsel from Old Testament professors.

I have read the text many times.

Last but never least, I have consulted the Holy Spirit.

What I gleaned has changed my life—even as I study and write this book you hold in your hands. The information is valuable, but the revelation from the Holy Spirit has been truly life-changing. Let's dive in.

WHY WISDOM LITERATURE STILL MATTERS

Job is part of a trilogy of Old Testament books focused on wisdom: Job, Ecclesiastes, and Proverbs. We quote Proverbs and Ecclesiastes all the time, but what about Job? We don't quote it that often.

Because of its depth and challenge, Job is referred to as *wisdom literature*.[1] In the ancient world, wisdom was considered a talent—highly valued and worth aspiring to. God

Himself was pleased when Solomon asked for wisdom over riches or power (1 Kings 3:10).

That's why I want to know what this book says, and I want to share it with you. I want to use the vast treasure chest of wisdom encapsulated in its forty-two chapters. Its contents house answers to some of the most asked questions of the Bible, including, but not limited to, why God allows "bad things to happen to good people." That alone makes Job worth the read.

While we cover many hard topics and questions in this book, our primary focus is the silence of God in the first thirty-eight chapters of the Book of Job, and most importantly, what happens when God *finally* speaks in chapter 38.

The date of the Book of Job is widely debated, but from my study, many scholars agree it is possibly the oldest book in the Bible. Clues such as Uz and Eliphaz—names that also appear in Genesis—suggest Job lived before the line of Israel was even established.

Some have questioned whether the Book of Job is fictional due to its extreme contents, but that theory falls apart fast, as Job—the person—is mentioned in other parts of Scripture. The prophet Ezekiel mentions Job in Ezekiel 14:14, 20, and Job is also mentioned in James 5:11: "We count those blessed who endured. You have heard of the endurance of Job, and have seen the outcome of the Lord's dealings, that the Lord is full of compassion and is merciful."

James is widely known as Jesus' brother; therefore, James's reference to Job would mean that Jesus and the Jewish people—both Christians and not—would've had a broad understanding of the Book of Job.

While the author is unknown, the style reads like a tantalizing drama that would make a good movie today. It's written in both prose and poetry, with the addition of dialogue and extremely dramatic monologues. (Yay!)

MEET JOB, MY BESTIE

OK, now that your eyes are glazed over from the background info—let's talk about Job, the man. Ahem (clearing my throat), allow me to introduce to you my best friend, Job. Job was a baller. (My words, not the scholars'; they are too spiritual for that.)

Job's name in Hebrew is *Iyyob*, meaning "hated or persecuted."[2] He lived in the land of Uz, a large territory east of Jordan. He was "blameless, upright, fearing God and turning away from evil" (Job 1:1). He had ten children—three daughters and seven sons—and he was married. Our boy was rich—like mega-rich. He had seven thousand sheep, three thousand camels, five hundred yoke of oxen, and five hundred female donkeys. Along with those he had many servants (Job 1:3). The Bible calls him the "greatest man in all the East." His kids got along too, which is nice—another blessing. They got along so well that they ate together at each other's house quite often.

Because Job was a righteous and upright man, after the sons and daughters dined together, he would offer burnt offerings for them on their behalf, thinking, "Perhaps my sons have sinned and cursed God in their hearts" (Job 1:5). This is quite interesting because it would have been before Moses instituted the Law. In the pre-Law period, the father of a household often served as family priest, offering sacrifices on behalf of his family (Gen. 15:9–10, 22:13). This offers another clue that Job's story predates Jewish tradition.

These facts give you a good understanding of who we are dealing with: a good guy—the best—who loves the Lord and is faithful and loyal to the Lord. Because of his righteousness, God blessed Job. While he sinned as we all do, he wasn't entangled in sin. He did right in the sight of God. This is important for you to know based on what's coming next. Here we go.

THE TUG OF WAR BETWEEN HEAVEN AND HELL

Satan has access to heaven, and a day came when Satan appeared before God. God asked where he had come from, and he answered, "From roaming about on the earth and walking around on it" (Job 1:7). This is probably why Peter references Satan as a "roaring lion" (1 Pet. 5:8). God's response to Satan was "Have you considered My servant Job?" After that God goes on to say: "For there is no one like him on the earth, a blameless and upright man, fearing God and turning away from evil" (Job 1:8).

Satan replies, "Does Job fear God for nothing?" Then, he talks about the hedge of protection that God has placed around Job. Satan tells God that, of course, Job is righteous and blameless because God has spoiled him. Satan whines about the fact that God blessed Job, insinuating that if God stopped protecting and blessing Job, he would definitely turn his back on Him. God then replies, "All that he has is in your power, only do not put forth your hand on him" (Job 1:12). When God gave Satan access to Job's stuff, Satan wasted no time. Shortly after that conversation, Satan did what he does best: destroy.

That same day Job's oxen were stolen by the Sabeans, fire burned the sheep, the Chaldeans raided the camels and took them, and all his sons and daughters were killed in a great windstorm that struck the house where they were eating.

One servant after another came and delivered this news "while he was still speaking" (Job 1:16).

OK, this is a lot.

Deep breath.

Deep cleansing breath.

I have more to tell you, but I want you to process for a minute all these horrific tragedies that happened simultaneously in Job's life. He went from wealthy—not just in possessions but also in legacy—to nothing. Immediate grief ensued. He lost almost everything with this first pass of Satan's destruction. This entire book will unpack these tragedies. I don't want to overwhelm you with speaking about all this information in chapter 1. We have already covered quite a lot for you to process, but I will say this: This was only Satan's first pass.

Yet, even after all this loss, Job didn't curse God. In fact, when the dust settled, his exact words were, "The LORD gave and the LORD has taken away. Blessed be the name of the LORD" (Job 1:21).

Because Job wouldn't surrender his faith, God allowed Satan to have a second attempt at him. God adds, "He still holds fast his integrity, although you incited Me against him to ruin him without cause" (Job 2:3). Satan responds, "Skin for skin! Yes, all that a man has, he will give for his life. However, reach out Your hand now, and touch his bone and his flesh; he will curse You to Your face!" (Job 2:4–5, NASB). Satan, with permission from God, "smote Job with sore boils from the sole of his foot unto his crown" (Job 2:7, KJV). Guess what? It didn't work. Job never cursed God.

SATAN IS AFTER YOUR FAITH

There is so much *rich* goodness to unpack, I can't wait to fully dive in. But first, I want to minister to those who find themselves in a place where God is silent and who are in a season of great loss. Just as Job was. God didn't speak to Job a single time during his loss. This is hard to hear, but it's true. He was silent. If you are in that season and God is silent, you are in the best company ever: Job's. Satan didn't care about Job's stuff; Satan's only objective was to get Job to surrender his faith. He is an opportunist. He wanted the tally of Job's life on his side of the board.

Satan fundamentally believed, based on the text, that the only reason that Job loved God and had faith in Him was because of his stuff. As proved in the dialogue between God and Satan, Satan thought that if Job's blessings were taken away, Job would fold his faith like a cheap lawn chair. Satan worked so hard for Job's faith because it's the only thing Satan doesn't have access to.

He knows that your faith can move mountains.

Your faith can heal.

Your faith can break the generational curses that have plagued you for years.

He knows that to access the power of God in your life, you must cash in the currency of your faith. Therefore, he wants your faith, and since he doesn't have access to it, it drives him crazy.

What's the only way for him to get it?

You have to surrender it.

He thinks that if he makes things bad enough for you, you will willingly depart from your most powerful weapon and protection: the shield of faith. Why does he want your faith so badly? Because it's the only thing that is eternal. It's the only thing that secures your spot in heaven. It's the only thing that will outlast this world. Everything else you will leave behind. It is the only thing that is more powerful than any arrow he produces to destroy you. So he works hard for it. It's precious to him.

He'll never be after temporal things. That will never be his goal. Temporal things are a means to an end for him. The goal is your faith. Whatever attack you may be facing, the goal is not that which was lost; it is for you to willingly give your faith up. Your faith is the target; your faith is his bullseye. Job shows us how strong the thing called faith can be—when exercised, it is the only thing that is impossible to please God without (Heb. 11:6). It's valuable. The enemy doesn't have access to it, so he works hard to steal it from you.

THE ENEMY WITHIN

Job's trials didn't come just from his losses; they also came from his own wife.

Job's wife is not named, and the text mentions her only one other time, in chapter 2, where Job asserts his integrity. Other than that, she has but one short yet loud moment in the text. She is not even mentioned at the end of the book.

After the loss of her ten children, her wealth, her possessions, and her status, Job's wife says this: "Do you still hold fast your integrity? Curse God and die!" (Job 2:9). Initially, I didn't think her role in Job's story was substantial enough to spend much time discussing it. However, my mind has changed as I have processed the depth of feeling coming from such an influential person in Job's life.

While Job had friend problems, he also had family problems—deep family problems. Perhaps you can relate. In my mind, Job's wife represents the unnamed family member who doesn't understand faith. Don't get me wrong, I have much empathy for Job's wife. She too suffered a severe trial because of her union with Job. But as she processed the loss, she decided that God had gone too far and being in relationship with Him was no longer worthwhile. She wrongly assumed God caused the loss, which likely led her to counsel Job to "curse God and die."

Both she and Job had seen their worst nightmare come to life, but the couple chose different paths. Job chose to cling to the Lord; his grief-stricken wife chose to forsake Him. Satan had drawn battle lines even in their marriage. Job's wife was so racked with grief that the thought of God disgusted her, and she wanted Job to curse Him, and then die.

She represents the reality of what can happen to us when great loss knocks on our door. Her words are sharp, even offensive, but their sentiment is common. Job's response is the exception; his wife's is the rule. Interestingly enough, Job gets close to doing just as his wife suggested. He cursed the day he was born, and he most definitely despised the fact that he was allowed to face what transpired. However, he stopped short of cursing God. Job questioned God, but he never cursed Him. Job was able to reject the temptation presented by his wife.

From the text we know that God allowed Satan to attack everything Job had except his life. That tells me Job's wife was probably a pawn in the enemy's scheme to get Job to surrender his faith. That's what Satan wanted, but he didn't have access to it. So if losing everything didn't break Job, the enemy would use his wife, the one closest to Job, to persuade him to fold. She was the enemy from within.

I don't blame her for being grief-stricken and thinking death would be better than the life Job was living. But I also see how Satan manipulated her grief and used it against her.

I write about Job's wife to caution you. The story is all too common. Great loss or trial hits a family, and those left reeling draw battle lines, sometimes against one another. One side may choose God while the other forsakes Him. Neither can find common ground due to the deep pain they've suffered. So they are at war. Thanksgiving is fraught with friction. Both sides are hurting, both need healing, both need each other, but an attack seems easier than an alliance. War seems more reasonable than making peace.

It may not be your spouse causing spiritual division; it could be your mom, your aunt, or your grandpa. No matter where the tension is coming from, it can be more damaging to your faith than the crisis that created the rift. Why? Because the ones opposing you know you best and love you most. Their voices are the ones that influence you more than the friends you have met along the way. These enemies within can make or break your faith, especially in a time when it is shaky at best. You aren't imagining the snide remarks and cutting looks. The enemy will influence any living vessel that lets him. Expect it. Don't be surprised by it. Plan for it. Watch for it. Be on guard. If the enemy can influence a family member, he's struck gold.

Job is quick with a wonderful, "stop the madness" response to his wife's words. He says, "'You speak as one of the foolish women speaks. Shall we indeed accept good from God and not accept adversity?'" (Job 2:10). Then we again see that "in all this Job did not sin with his lips" (Job 2:10).

Job is resolute. Not only is he going to follow the Lord; he will follow the Lord no matter what—even in the face of opposition from his own wife. Job's response is one we can take to Thanksgiving dinner. We too can say that no matter what happens, we will choose the Lord.

After that word from Job, we hear nothing more from

his wife. If you follow in his footsteps, you'll find that you too can shut down the assault on your faith from the enemy within your family.

SATAN ACCUSED JOB OF BEING GOOD

Satan is the great accuser and stands before God, day and night, accusing us (Rev. 12:10). It's interesting to me that he doesn't just accuse us of doing something bad; he accuses us before God of doing good. He twists our good, righteous lives, and before God, tries to convince Him that though we may be good, our motives are bad—that we only choose to do good because God blesses us, not because we love Him.

The enemy told God that Job had faith and did good only because of what God had done for him. Satan assumed he knew Job's limit, and he assumes he knows yours too.

Surely, Job wouldn't stay righteous if God stopped blessing him. So God allowed the blessings to stop. Why would God do that? Well, some reasons we know, and some we will never know. But one reason is clear: to show the enemy—and us today—just how much faith can endure. Faith can transcend tragedy. Faith can transcend health diagnoses. Faith can even transcend the loss of a loved one—even that of a child. Faith can weather rejection from friends or even a spouse. Faith in our able God is stronger than anything we face on earth. It even transcends seasons where we most need to hear from God and He is silent.

Let me enlighten you: You may not be facing what you're facing now because you are being "punished," as some incomplete theology might suggest. It could be that God sees the depth of your faith in this moment. You are His prize. He knows what you can and will endure. He sees your faith capacity. You do not, but He has measured how durable it is. The Lord is sending a message to the accuser that he can't have you.

He wants to show the enemy that you were never up for grabs as a pawn in his plan. Your faith is deep and wide, substantial and impenetrable by what you are facing. Satan hates the faithful. God baited the enemy to fail when he selected you for this season. He did the same with His Son, Jesus. He did the same with Paul. He did the same with the eleven disciples who clung to their faith. The enemy who baits us to sin was baited by God and took the bait.

God loves the faithful. He sees the depth of the faith you have. *There is nothing the Lord loves more than you, nothing that makes Him prouder than your faith,* and nothing that Satan hates more than your faith. Your faith has gotten you recognized in the throne room of heaven. Job was handpicked for this moment. Jesus, for His; David, for his; Paul, for his; and you, for yours.

Rest assured: Satan will be held accountable for these things (just look at the last chapter of Job). But for now, sweet, weary warrior, let's get through what you are facing together. Let's face the silence together. Let's overcome together. We have a reward to claim. The enemy just overplayed his hand.

When I stood from my bed that night, I heard a flashing message in my spirit, "Do you remember Me?" I walked to the room across from my bedroom and boldly, assertively said to the Lord, "You better speak, because if You don't, I won't make it." I opened my Bible and read the words in Psalm 91:14–16 (NIV): "'Because he loves me,' says the LORD, 'I will rescue him; I will protect him, for he acknowledges My name. He will call on Me, and I will answer him; I will be with him in trouble, I will deliver him and honor him. With long life I will satisfy him and show him My salvation.'"

I knew then that God would get the final word in my circumstance—and friend, He has. Spoiler alert: He did in Job's, and He will in yours too.

FUN ANNOUNCEMENT!

Throughout this book, you'll notice QR codes such as the following one. Each code links to a short video message from me, where I'll share encouragement and dive deeper into the truths you're reading. You'll find a new QR code at the end of every chapter. Think of these videos as a way for me to walk with you on this journey, reminding you that you are not alone and that you have my full support as you grow in God.

Scan this QR code or visit AutumnMilesBooks.com/ holyghosted/resources to watch a brief video from me with encouragement and deeper insight for your journey.

Chapter 2
HOLY SILENCE—THE
SOUND OF SILENCE

*My God, my God, why have You forsaken me? Far
from my help are the words of my groaning. My
God, I cry out by day, but You do not answer; and
by night, but I have no rest. Yet You are holy, You
who are enthroned upon the praises of Israel.*
—Psalm 22:1–3, nasb

I T WAS COLD outside, and the extra-long golf cart I was
riding in offered no shelter from the wind and rain that
February Saturday in Waco, Texas. I shivered multiple
times, trying to listen to the young, well-spoken man from
admissions to Baylor University. Eddie and I had made the
trek from Dallas with our daughter, Grace, to Waco to tour
Baylor as one of her potential colleges. The dreary condi-
tions of the day matched my attitude about Grace attending
the school—not because I had anything bad to say about
Baylor but quite the opposite. I had many friends who loved
the school and highly recommended it for Grace. But I knew
what God had told me: Three years earlier, loud and clear,
He said that she wouldn't be attending Baylor.

Grace sat up with her back straight, fully engaged with the
boy from admissions. I don't know whether it was because

23

he was a cutie or she was genuinely interested in what he had to say. Either way, it was clear: She was ready to attend. She had told me back when she was a freshman in high school that she would go to Baylor, and every move she had made up to that point supported it.

Grace was the mascot for our entire school district throughout high school. She was extremely good at it—so good, in fact, that she had won awards and was even hired by the National Cheerleading Association to teach her mascot skills. With that experience she planned to represent Baylor, if so chosen, as the Baylor Bear mascot. I had taken her to Baylor a few times over the years for mascot workshops to help her prepare for tryouts, and every time I drove her there, I suppressed the clear message the Lord gave me that she wouldn't attend Baylor.

On the return trip from one of the mascot workshops, Grace looked at me while I was driving and said, "Mom, please tell me what you really think about me going to Baylor. I can tell you're hesitant." I stared at the road, gripped the steering wheel, and silently cried out to the Lord. My daughter was staring at me, longing for a much-needed stamp of approval on the future she believed was already hers. I asked the Lord, "Why are You having me be silent on this? Why can't I tell her that she won't attend? Can I tell her now?"

This had gone on long enough. She was desperate for my blessing, and I only wanted to calm her heart and give it to her. To God, I begged, "Please let me share with her what You have shared with me." To Grace, I was silent, but my voice was heard in heaven. My plea to the Lord was answered with a "Not yet." I could sense the pause in my spirit from the Lord. Even though I had been silent on this topic with

Grace for nearly three years, it wasn't time to speak quite yet.

What Grace didn't know was that when the Lord told me she wouldn't go to Baylor, He had also told me to remain silent about it until further notice. That command broke my heart. I went back and forth with God over it. I hated it. It felt dishonest—like I was playing some game with my daughter. I knew I wasn't deceiving her. I was responding in faith to a task the Lord had given me as a mom, but man was it a hard one. I disagreed with the ask, but I didn't dare disobey.

I'm a mom of four, and we've always cultivated a culture of open communication in our home. We are honest with one another. Eddie and I have taught our kids, from a young age, that they can tell us anything—and that it'll be met with grace and truth. This felt like a betrayal of that very culture—a betrayal to *myself*, in some ways, too. The silence felt like I was concealing something Grace needed.

But I also knew this fact: Eddie and I are intentional about the kind of children we are raising. We are raising warriors for the Lord. We are raising children who will be on the front line of kingdom battles, as generals in God's army. Therefore, if God Himself told me to "stay silent until I give you the freedom to share," then I could only trust that He knew something I didn't. He was parenting her through my obedience. My emotions needed to get out of the way so God could do what *He* needed to do in her heart.

I was torn—torn between my love for Grace and my desire to affirm her and bring her peace, and my unshakable trust in God, who asked me to remain silent for reasons I didn't understand.

By this point I had walked intimately with God long enough to submit all my questions and disagreements to Him. I knew that somewhere in the silence was a process, a maturation of her faith, and a forming of her character. God needed me to stay out of it. My silence, for three years, was an act of pure faith. If silence was what God wanted to use as His tool to teach Grace—more than my earthly need to comfort her—I would follow His order for her life and wait expectantly for Him to bring forth the fruit.

That night, as Grace stared at me with her big, longing blue eyes, I simply said, "Grace, let's just see what God does." She turned away and stared at the road, deflated. She didn't know the war raging inside me; she didn't know the why. But she let out a big sigh—one that felt like it belonged to both of us. It seemed to say, "I don't like this process, but I guess I don't have a choice."

The day in the golf cart came months later—February of her senior year—when the pressure was on. Her friends had already chosen schools for the fall, and she was left with no progress in her plans. I was getting anxious about God moving, and I felt like we were running out of time. I was prayerfully tapping my foot, wondering whether that day would be the day when I could speak up and give her the message God had given me.

After the school tour ended, we wandered into the Baylor gift shop. I pretended to browse the merch. Grace, of course, wanted an entire outfit that was nothing but Baylor gear. I bought the outfit begrudgingly, knowing it would go unused. But again, the Lord hadn't released me to speak, so I maintained my vow of silence. I trusted only in His nature as my reason.

What Do We Do with God's Silence?

Just as I was silent with Grace for three years in a tough season of her life, God was silent to Job for thirty-eight chapters. Yes, you read that right: God was completely silent and didn't say a single word to Job for almost the entire book. Let me remind you: Satan had taken all ten of his children—they were dead along with his entire livelihood, his health, his marriage. Now the enemy was after Job's mind. There wasn't one word from God, not a single word. Nothing. Silence.

Given Job's horrific circumstances, it is understandable that our culture—and maybe even we ourselves—find God's silence unacceptable. How dare God not say one word to Job? How mean can God be? The self-righteous spirit of the Pharisees will begin to swell in us if we imagine this man suffering so viciously with no consolation from God. If we're not careful, we will begin to judge God: We judge His character, assume His absence, then pick apart His promises and stamp them null and void.

In a world that looks at constant access to communication as some badge of honor, divine silence defies the unwritten rules of our society and deems God irrelevant. We would cancel God in our minds as a heartless dictator, celebrating our negligible communication skills instead. In turn, we would become the compassionate demigods all should worship, praising the pious comfort of our speech to the individual we have decided requires it, and we would render God foolish.

Culture has made silence a type of violence. It's not just rude anymore; it's criminal not to speak. Under this warped barometer of righteousness, do we also render God a criminal for His selected silence? Silence, in our culture, breaks the social law of self-indulgence. We can't stand it. It's hard to take. It demands self-control and sacrifice on our part—and dare I say, a deeper level of faith that isn't quite ripe yet.

Silence is uncomfortable. It makes our senses shriek in agony. We demand to be addressed just to ease the awkwardness.

Yes, culture has pastored us in heresy. The shepherdless have shepherded us, and we have taken notes from their sermon. If we're not careful, we may start applying them as fact. I was tempted to adopt this culturally acceptable view while God asked me to stay silent with my daughter. It felt wrong. It felt like I was being more compassionate than God. It felt like I cared more than He did. I was tempted to get trapped in a prison of self-righteousness.

That—right there—is exactly the perspective Satan wants you to take. He wants to dominate the vacuum God's silence has allowed in this season. Satan wants to fill it. He is ever so happy to fill the stillness with all sorts of noise. Satan wants nothing more than to pastor you during this season of silence from God. Ugh, that sentence makes me shiver with disgust, but it's true.

He is ready with thoughts, ideas, other people's opinions—and more than anything, he wants you to ask questions. He wants you to question yourself, your upbringing, God's character, the Word of God, and most of all, he wants you to question your faith. The silence leaves a void, and he will try to fill it any way you let him.

He is ready to swoop in and whisper, "Do you remember that addiction that served you for years? That thing you got rid of because you got to know Jesus? Let's go back to that. It'll make you feel better while God is silent."

Satan is an opportunist when God decides to be silent. Like culture, he wants you to judge God.

I'm writing this book as a response to where our minds can go when God is silent—especially in what seems like the moment we *most* need to hear from Him. In the following chapters, we will unpack questions such as, "What do we do in a season of silence?" Together, we will explore how *not* to assume what God is doing during times of severe trial. We have to watch what we think.

We will also tackle some of the most scandalous questions I believe every Christian has, even if not everyone is brave enough to ask. We will also chat about what Satan is *really* after when the Holy Spirit seems to ghost us during our hardest seasons.

THE SILENCE CAUSES JOB TO LOSE HIS MIND A LITTLE

For now, however, let's get into the silence from God. Silence from God is one of the most maddening things in the Christian life. After all, we are bought in. We know we need God's voice. We have already signed up for a relationship with Him—a two-way one at that. So had Job. He loved God. He was allegiant to the Lord alone, as we can see from his character. He wanted to hear from God.

After the day when all hell broke loose in his life and God was silent, Job talks about it. He says, "If I called and He answered me, I could not believe that He was listening to my voice" (Job 9:16). Oof, Job was starting to lose it. He was a little salty. He was saying that he didn't even believe that God would answer him because he didn't believe God was truly listening to him. Ouch, Job.

Reading this feels like an old, cringeworthy Facebook post where a woman publicly outs her husband for having an affair. It is raw and feels a little inappropriate. But honestly? I've felt just like that. Have you? Yep, we are just as cringeworthy as Job, but he just had the guts to say it aloud.

Here is another cringeworthy line from our boy Job about God's silence: "Why do You hide Your face and consider me Your enemy?" (Job 13:24). Job was beginning to assume things about God's silence that just weren't true. He didn't just question; he started to assume lies about God. That, my friend, is exactly what Satan wants us to do when we are seeking a word from the Lord and can't seem to find it.

Job, like us, began to attach his intellect, though feeble, to something above him: the mysterious ways of God. He has moved, in this verse, from anger to assumptions, which ultimately reveals his growing impatience. We all know the verse—God's ways are higher than our ways (Isa. 55:8)—yet when we disagree with how He chooses to move, we start trying to make sense of it all by assuming we *know* what God is doing. In Job's case he began to believe that God considered him as an enemy.

The next shift in Job is the most human of all: longing. He moved from anger to impatience to a deep, aching desire to simply hear God's voice. Listen to what he said: "Oh that I knew where I might find Him, that I might come to His seat! I would present my case before Him and fill my mouth with arguments. I would learn the words which He would answer, and perceive what He would say to me" (Job 23:3–5).

This statement makes me sad. Can you hear the longing in his voice? There was no more anger—no accusations, no assumptions. He no longer needed to know *why* God was silent; he just wanted to hear from Him. Job wanted to hear the sweet, life-giving voice of his Lord. He longed to find out where God was. He was like a son looking for their father's comfort and couldn't seem to get it. Nothing mattered more to him than hearing the comforting voice of the One he trusted. At this point in the text, God's voice is all Job wants. He didn't ask for his stuff back. He didn't beg for revenge. He just wanted to sit at the Comforter's feet and *hear* His voice again.

GOD MAY SEEM SILENT, BUT HE ISN'T

Job was feeling the effects of silence: mentally, emotionally, and spiritually. But was God actually silent? The answer is no. While God didn't interject in the dialogue for most of the Book of Job, Job didn't know that God was actually talking about him in heaven. Heaven talked about Job. Heaven *knew* who Job was.

Conversations in the throne room between God and Satan happened—conversations Job never heard. No, God didn't speak directly to Job, but does it help you to know that while God was silent *to* Job, He was not silent *about* him?

Let's look at it:

> The LORD said to Satan, "From where do you come?" Then Satan answered the LORD and said, "From roaming about on the earth and walking around on it." The LORD said to Satan, "Have you considered My servant Job? For there is no one like him on the earth, a blameless and upright man, fearing God and turning away from evil."
>
> —JOB 1:7–8

Job hadn't heard this statement from the Lord. He had no idea that God and Satan were having a conversation about his righteousness. God told Satan that there was "no one like him on earth." WHAT? Excuse me? What an amazing statement—made by God Himself. (Wow.)

Satan replied, as if to say, "Yep, I know he's righteous—but that's only because You have been so good to him." Then, "Satan answered the LORD. 'Does Job fear God for nothing?'" (Job 1:9).

Satan continued to talk about the blessing and protection of the Lord on Job's life (Job 1:10). After this, God permitted Satan to test Job. When Satan goes out and does his worst, *another* conversation occurs in heaven. The test didn't work. Job didn't "curse God." So God again offered Job as a suggestion to Satan. In Job 2:3, He repeats, "There is no one like him in all the earth, a blameless and upright man, fearing God and turning away from evil."

This time, Satan was permitted to touch Job's health. Let that sink in: Job had been through something no one should ever have to go through—and while God wasn't speaking *to* Job, He was speaking *about* Job to the entire throne room. He was boasting about Job's blamelessness. All heaven was overhearing God Himself talk about how special Job was.

Heaven was talking *about* Job, even when it wasn't talking *to* Job.

In my season of silence with my daughter, I was talking to heaven about her. I was praying—almost daily—about her need to hear from us. She didn't know my internal wrestle, but God did. I recently spoke to Grace about that season in her life and the silence from me. She admitted that it was "extremely frustrating." But she also had no idea I was talking to heaven about it regularly. She even said it would've eased her discomfort if she had known I was constantly checking in with God about her.

Does it comfort you that even in a season of silence, heaven isn't silent about *you*?

God didn't even use Job's last name. He referred to him as simply Job. Job was so recognizable in heaven that no other identifying factors were needed. He was known by his first name in the courts of heaven—and as soon as God said Job, Satan and all heaven knew exactly who He meant.

Job was *famous* in heaven.

I believe this would've calmed Job's heart. I know it calms mine—in the seemingly never-ending seasons of silence. Heaven's view of us changes how we perceive earth's disappointments.

GOD MONITORS OUR SITUATION CLOSELY, EVEN WHEN HE IS SILENT

Even when God is silent, He monitors our situation. God put Satan on a leash. There were clear limits to how far Satan could test Job. In Job 1:12 the Lord defined those parameters: "Then the LORD said to Satan, 'Behold, all that he has is in your power; only do not put forth your hand on him.' So Satan departed from the presence of the LORD."

There were boundaries—Satan couldn't lay a single finger on Job. His body and life were off-limits. When Satan was allowed to test Job a second time, God spoke up again and set new boundaries to limit what the enemy could do. Job 2:6 says, "So the LORD said to Satan, 'Behold, he is in your power, only spare his life.'"

This time Satan was allowed to access his health. While I know it's hard to grasp why God would allow any access at all (trust me, we will discuss that later), this shows us something powerful: God was monitoring the situation carefully. He was still in control. He never abandoned Job to chaos. Even when He wasn't speaking *to* Job, He was setting boundaries for Satan and keeping the leash tight.

Job had no idea. Isn't that like us? We don't realize that God is actively protecting us behind the scenes. He doesn't always explain how He's intervening. But the enemy can't touch us unless God permits it. If He does allow it, there's a limit—a red line that the enemy can't cross. God monitors it carefully to ensure the enemy obeys His limits.

This comforts me again. God knows us intimately. He watches us so closely that He ensures what we face won't crush us. It doesn't mean that it isn't hard. It can feel absolutely debilitating. It doesn't mean that it won't feel impossible. You might be staring down your situation right now, thinking, "I see no way out of this." But even when it *feels* like too much, His power makes up the difference. He monitors every trial that we walk. He is aware of every hard thing in our lives. He has put the enemy on a leash. He can't come at you any harder than God allows.

Does it give you solace to know that though silence abounds, God's eyes are on *everything*?

For whatever reason, my four kids flock to me. I can't go into another room without them trailing behind me. My husband does the same. All five of them want to be near me constantly. If I dare leave a room, they'll ask, "Why are you leaving us? Mom, where are you going?" They act as if I have offended them by having the audacity to leave their presence. I used to think this would fade as the kids got older. I mean, seriously? Who wants to be around their mom 100 percent of the time?

That's when it hit me. I realized my presence alone settles them. They don't even need me to talk to them. Nope, they just want to know I am in the room with them.

There is something powerful about that. They don't need me to speak, but they like the security of knowing I am watching over everything. My presence is more powerful than my words. Proximity brings more peace than my words. I can be silent in the room, yet the room will be at peace because I am there—quietly monitoring. This makes their hearts relax.

This is precisely what God does for us. He wants to comfort your heart by offering a view from heaven that you may never have considered. His presence is more powerful than words. He is in the room, monitoring everything, even when He doesn't say a word.

One of the most beautiful things about the Book of Job is that we're given a rare view from heaven. We get a peek behind the curtain of the supernatural realm—something we rarely consider when God is silent. But it exists. It's real. A. W. Tozer wrote in *The Pursuit of God* that the supernatural world is *more* of a reality than the temporal world we live in.[1] It existed before we existed and will be here long after the world ends; it is more of a reality than what we see on this side of heaven.

I believe this is why the passage in Job 1 is there for us to glean from: It's heaven's perspective. The Book of Job reminds us that God isn't distant, detached, or indifferent. He is watching, He is present, and He is setting boundaries to protect us, even when we can't hear Him.

You can rest in that truth and allow your heart to relax.

SILENCE PRODUCES ANTICIPATION

I previously pointed out in this chapter that Job moves through the process of God's silence. He begins with anger, moves to questions and assumptions, and then eventually lands in a place of longing to hear from God. Nothing else mattered to him anymore. Job becomes utterly focused on God alone due to the silence. Silence from God, while confusing and often painful, creates a longing—a sharpened anticipation to hear from Him that purifies us.

God once told me, "Sometimes I silence Myself because when I speak, I want you to listen." In elongated seasons of silence, we hone in on one thing: hearing from God. Time has a way of producing purity in what we seek for comfort.

Our friends' and family's voices aren't powerful enough.

Their words fall flat. It almost gets to a point where you'd rather they didn't speak because they don't fully understand the trial you're facing. Can you relate? Their words aren't equipped with the perspective God's are. It's easy to become annoyed at someone else's feeble attempt to comfort you. Most are well-meaning, yes, but they are of no use.

Let me remind you: You don't need their words; you need God's. You may be in a season right now where the trial has hit you so deep that their words are too shallow. That's where God wants you to be, longing for Him alone. Because, my dear friend, when He speaks—and He will—it will be so powerful that it will change your life forever. The word He will give to you will have His glory attached. It will be a Rhema word, or a perfect word, in due season.

Those words from God are worth the wait.

Exactly one month after that trip to Waco, Texas, to Baylor University, I traveled to Liberty University to teach Women's Leadership classes as a guest lecturer. When my assistant was booking my airplane tickets, God spoke to me and said, "Grace will go with you." This wasn't a suggestion; it was a command. I rarely get commands. I have before, but I knew this one would be pivotal for her future. I immediately called Grace and told her she needed to attend the trip with me.

Let me give you some context. Grace had already made it crystal clear that she would *not* be attending Liberty. Since Eddie and I are alumni, she didn't want us to pressure her, so we didn't. But she agreed to come with me on this trip. The moment we stepped foot on the campus, I knew in my spirit: This was where God wanted her. But I said nothing. I stayed silent.

Grace began to meet college kids that day. Her demeanor clearly softened toward the school, but I didn't bring it up and made sure that I said nothing. When we boarded the plane home, I finally asked her what she thought about the school. All she said was, "I liked it." That was it. She gave me nothing else. Just a simple, bland, "I liked it." I thought, "That's all I get? Boo!"

That same week Grace went to the youth service at our church, and the Spirit of the living God began to speak to her. During her small group, she asked for prayer about where she should attend college. The group prayed over her. At the end of the night, the youth pastor got up and said something to the effect of, "This is off topic, but I feel like there is someone in this room who needs to go home and ask their parents where they need to attend college." Grace knew that God Himself was talking to her about her future. She knew that she was supposed to go to Liberty University. God had spoken to her while I remained silent.

I will never forget her walking into our home that night. She flopped on our gray, velvet chair that sits opposite our bed and said nothing. I looked at her and asked, "Baby, are you OK?" She told me about the events of that evening, such as how the youth pastor said, "Go home and ask your parents where they think you should attend college." There was a long pause in the room. Then she looked at me and asked, "Mom, where do you think God wants me to go?"

As soon as the words left her lips, the Spirit of God screamed at me and said, *"Now. Tell her now."* I knew this was the time to tell her all God had told me. I immediately began crying—due to the long wait and the relief that the directive of the Lord had just given me. I told her, "I believe that God wants you at Liberty University."

Do you know what she said?

"God told me that too. He told me that tonight. I heard Him clearly."

That moment marked a shift. Through miraculous circumstances, she is now attending Liberty University.

As I've processed this situation with Grace over the past two years, I've realized why I needed to be silent for so long. My silence was necessary for her to get a Rhema word from God. God didn't want her to depend on my word any longer; He was training her to rely on His word. My obedience to the silence allowed Grace to hear from God first before she confirmed what He said to me. As she left our home to begin life on her own, God wanted to be the voice she relied on from now on, not mine. This situation allowed for that. She clearly heard from God first; His word changed her life.

My friend, while the silence is very real, there is immense purpose in it—a purpose that can be hard to discern at times. He will use the hardest seasons of our lives to allow us to train our minds to search for His voice alone. No one else's voice matters. Whatever the reason for your season of silence, I know a few things: (1) you'll probably have some questions and assumptions that we'll need to work through, and (2) you'll need a way to navigate this journey without losing faith.

The following two chapters will be your best friend as you learn how to walk the journey of silence until God breaks it. I adore you, friend. Hang in there. I pray this chapter felt like a warm hug and gave you some insight to help you carry on.

Scan this QR code or visit AutumnMilesBooks.com/holyghosted/resources to watch a brief video from me with encouragement and deeper insight for your journey.

Chapter 3
HOLY CHARACTER—THE CHARACTER OF GOD IS THE BACKBONE FOR SILENCE

This God—his way is perfect; the word of the Lord proves
true; he is a shield for all those who take refuge in him.
—PSALM 18:30, ESV

I LAY IN MY bed completely still, eyes wide open. The house was silent. I turned my head slightly to glance at the clock; it was 4:06 a.m. The time seemed to shout at me, "You need to stay in bed and rest." But my racing, pounding heart wouldn't allow it. It was at war with the rest that I desperately needed.

My thoughts began to scream the name of Jesus over and over: "Jesus, Jesus, Jesus, Jesus, help me." I said His name repeatedly, waiting for the relief I was sure it would provide. At some point, while repeating His name, I drifted back to sleep. The name of Jesus was the only thing that had the power to calm my spirit.

Around 5 a.m., my racing heart and mind woke me up once again as if to remind me: Anxiety owned me. I was a slave, powerless to escape its harsh demands.

Quietly, I removed the blanket and slid my exhausted legs to the side of the bed, careful not to wake my snoring husband. My fight-or-flight response had kicked in. I needed to get out of that room. I needed to get out of the house. I needed air—fresh air. I needed relief, but I couldn't seem to find it.

My thoughts began to spiral, and these questions inevitably arose: "Where is my relief?" "God, where are You?" "Why can't I find You anywhere?" "Why don't I have peace?" "When will this anxiety stop?" "Will it ever stop?" It felt like a prison that I couldn't escape.

I took advantage of the rare silence in the house, because with four children that kind of quiet is a luxury, and I slipped on my shoes. As I exited the bedroom, my pace quickened, as if to get my body out of the house as quickly as possible. I paused only to shush my dog and then slowly opened the back door. The burst of fresh air felt like medication for my racing heart.

I collapsed onto the weathered sectional couch that, in some ways, had become my safe haven. A cloud of dust shot out of the old cushions as the weight of my body hit them. The dust aggravated my allergies and made me sneeze— right as I burst into tears. I sat stiffly, back straightened, and fingers clenched to the cushion beneath me, and I sobbed.

After several minutes, my tears subsided. The rhythmic sound of the wind chime caught my attention, distracting me from the abnormal rhythm of my heart. Its gentle music offered a welcomed pause to my thoughts. I sat there for what seemed like an hour, hypnotized by the peaceful song of hope it was playing for me. My mind needed the distraction. For a brief time, my ruminating thoughts took a break.

My anxiety had been out of control for a little over a year. Looking back, I realize I was in shock. In 2020 I lost what seemed like every bit of momentum I had built in my work, and our business came to the brink of failure. Within one week my entire year was canceled. If that wasn't enough,

Eddie and I faced one of the biggest challenges our marriage had ever encountered. I had just released two books back-to-back and was still recovering from the burnout of travel.

Oh yes, and then that little thing called the COVID-19 pandemic happened.

Suddenly, I was also a homeschooling mom of two kindergarteners, a sixth grader, and an eighth grader. Cool, that was just what my anxiety needed.

The sudden shock threw me into a state of mind that I couldn't escape. I tried everything, but anxiety had my mind in a chokehold.

Was I praying? Yes, I was desperately praying!

Was I reading the Word of God? *Yes.* Every day, I pored over the pages of Scripture, hunting for the freedom I knew they offered.

Were any of these working?

It didn't seem like it.

I couldn't seem to find God. I couldn't feel Him. The pages of His precious Word were speaking, but I couldn't seem to receive their promises. Since becoming a Spirit-filled believer, I had never experienced this to such an extent. Yes, silent seasons had come before, but being unable to perceive the Lord anywhere was completely foreign. I was scared.

Lies had become more believable than truth.

The lies of my anxiety convinced me that every demonic thought that dropped into my head was fact—and that it was going to happen. It felt imminent. The monster of anxiety overpowered everything I read in Scripture. It was my boss. It was my Goliath, and it taunted me day in and day out.

I knew God was with me, but His precious, peaceful, life-giving voice—the one I lived for—was silent. I was looking so hard, and I was miserable, but my mind wouldn't quiet enough to give His voice room for the revelation I so desperately needed.

At the back of our home, we are surrounded by beautiful trees and a hillside of bushes that bloom and produce the most lush, green oasis—especially in the spring and summer. That morning, as the wind chime sang over me, I noticed the trees and bushes swaying to the same rhythm that powered the wind chime. They were at peace.

The wind and the trees began preaching to me, and the sermon they gave convinced me.

The first point in their three-point sermon: the faithfulness of God.

Winter had traumatized them to the point of near-death, and yet, God—in His faithfulness—had revived them.

My mind began to drift to the jealousy I felt for the trees. I coveted their peace. They didn't have anxiety. They didn't worry whether God would feed them. They simply let Him do it.

Caught up in my jealousy, I listened as they moved to the second and third points of their sermon: the consistency of God and His provision.

The seasons change, but God stays consistent. He had kept all those trees and bushes alive for years without their help, consistently providing them the elements they needed to sustain life. If they needed water, it rained. If sunshine was required, it appeared. If storms were needed to strengthen their roots, then so it would be.

Sadly, the sermon of the trees was interrupted by my own frustration and annoyance. These were the most elementary truths about God—and suddenly they were becoming *revelatory* to me.

I had preached this stuff for years. I knew all these things and had lived them. I had written books about them. Not one thing was new to me. I could give you all the verses to support the sermon from the trees. Although I had studied these truths for years, amid my anxiety, they were hard to receive.

As if the anxiety wasn't enough at that moment, I felt embarrassed. It seemed like the trees had more faith than I did.

The truth? They did.

I had known the intimacy of God for years. He was—and is—my best friend. There was no place I would rather be than in His presence. But that morning His presence was unperceivable.

This preacher girl had to admit, in the still-dark hours of the morning, that I couldn't hear Him. I couldn't feel Him.

As I stared at the trees that morning, I realized that what once worked—prayer, worship, and the Word—for whatever reason wasn't working in that season. I needed a fresh perspective on how to continue relying on the Lord.

Interestingly, my anxiety was pushing me to a deeper level with the Lord—not just a temporary depth I had tapped into during crises before but to a sustained depth—one I hadn't experienced for months and months, with no relief in sight.

Somewhere within me, courage began to stir.

A fight began to rise.

I always say, "Don't let the blonde hair fool you—I have a lion inside." That day she began to wake up from her slumber. Eyes still fixed on the trees, I realized they were preaching a sermon I hadn't heard before. It was new. It was delightfully fresh. A revelation—delivered through the sway of their leaves.

They spoke to me about God's faithfulness, His consistency, and His provision, but the most significant point in the orator of creation's message was the following:

God's character can be relied on in every stage of life—even the stages where God is entirely silent in your greatest time of need.

The trees preached about the character of God in the absence of His presence. Maybe I was having a little trouble locating God's presence just then, but I knew I could take His character to the bank. It was tangible. I had experienced it. Through every season God Himself had proved to me who He was and what His character is.

I experienced His character when I was delivered from my abusive marriage. In that season He was my merciful Father. He parented me with mercy and love I had never known.

I experienced His character when I met my husband, Eddie. God's provision was so tangible. I couldn't believe that the Lord had given me such an amazing man—someone so gracious—not intimidated by my past but willing to embrace it as part of me.

I experienced His character with the birth of my first daughter, when I was so weak and sick that I didn't know whether I would survive. God healed me. He was so compassionate and walked me through that dangerous pregnancy.

I experienced His character in our two adoptions. God's patience carried me through that hard season of waiting. I was so frustrated that we had to wait so long, and yet He never—not once—rebuked me for my impatience.

I experienced His character when I gave birth to my son, Jude; Eddie and I were all alone, two thousand miles away from our nearest family member when Jude came into the world. The Lord loved us and gave us the grace we needed to make it through. As I sat there that morning, I realized God's character, like a tapestry, had been woven into every single facet of my life. These were examples of how His character has never failed me and my family, but I could've thought of thousands of examples. My mind began to race. Yes—I can rely on God's character. I don't have to feel His presence to know His character will never change and will be faithful to me. My circumstances do not change God's character, nor do my fleeting feelings.

That was when the lion inside me began awakening.

YOU CAN TRUST GOD'S CHARACTER

In a season of long silence from God, you can rely on His character.

It is this truth that Job knew so well. During the crushing of his livelihood, his children, his wealth, his health, his friendships, and even his mental health, he knew that when all else failed, he could depend on what he knew about God's character. In this chapter and the following, I will focus on how we endure when facing God's silence. One way is knowing the character of God, which we will cover in this chapter. The other is knowing the Word of God, which we will cover in the following chapter.

Job's relationship with the Lord didn't rely on feeling God's presence—or even receiving a fresh word from Him. Job's relationship with God was grounded in one truth that Satan's lies couldn't penetrate: the character of God. Even when Job couldn't feel the Lord's presence or perceive that He was near, he trusted in who God had always proved Himself to be.

Job admitted his disorientation, when he said,

> Behold, I go forward, but He is not there, and back-
> ward, but I cannot perceive Him; when He acts on
> the left, I cannot behold Him; He turns on the right,

> I cannot see Him. But He knows the way I take;
> when He has tried me, I shall come forth as gold.
> —JOB 23:8–10

This is exactly how I felt. I couldn't find or perceive the Lord, but I knew that He was there. Like Job, I reminded myself that, while I couldn't locate God, He knew exactly where I was.

This was the reassurance I needed that morning: I can't feel You, but I know You are here. I can't see what You are doing, but I know I can rely on what I know about Your character.

Satan couldn't talk Job out of relying on God's character. We see proof of this in the text. Our first reference to Job's reliance on God's character may be the most famous verse in Job: "Though He slay me, I will hope in Him. Nevertheless, I will argue my ways before Him" (Job 13:15).

At this point in the story, Job has lost every single thing he had except his life. His life is in complete shambles. His wife was mocking him, and his friends—full of self-righteousness—their counsel was offensive to him. Oh yes, and let's not forget—he was sitting in ashes, covered in boils, and scraping himself with broken pieces of pottery. (Cool.)

Even then, Job clung to what he knew. The character of God was more real to him than the loss that surrounded him. Job wasn't leaning on what he had read or what he once felt—he was leaning on what he had experienced.

Like mine, Job's experiences with God throughout his life preached songs of hope to his temporal circumstances. God's goodness had walked with him through the early days of his life and through seasons of provision and blessing. The same God who had given him oxen, camels, sheep, donkeys, and blessed all the work of his hands was tangible in Job's life (Job

1:3). He saw facets of God's faithfulness in raising his seven sons and three daughters (Job 1:2). He valued the mercy of God so much that, when his children's feasting ended, Job would rise early and offer burnt offerings for each of them "just in case," saying, "Perhaps my sons have sinned and cursed God in their hearts" (Job 1:5). Job knew God—not just as an idea or a theology; he knew His ways. His entire life was built on the firm, dependable character of God.

Here's what's wild: This unimaginable suffering didn't come in the early years of Job's life, when he was spiritually green and still figuring things out. It came later, when Job was seasoned—when he had walked with God long enough to see the consistency in His mercy, His discipline, and His provision. So when the silence hit, when his world fell apart, Job didn't bow out. He didn't "curse God and die," as his wife so bluntly suggested (Job 2:9). He couldn't leave. His experience with God was too powerful to deny. Nothing was worth abandoning the God he knew.

The phrase "Though he slay me" (Job 13:15) is basically Job saying, "Even if He allows me to die—even if the worst happens—I won't stop trusting the Lord."

Even if God never restores what's been lost, I'll still trust Him.

Even if it's the end of me, I'll still trust Him.

He wouldn't stop. He couldn't. He had experienced the most incredible force on this side of heaven—the unmatched character of God. Satan even knew that Job would be a hard faith case to conquer, which is why he was hesitant to attack him in the beginning. Would it be worth Satan's while? Even Satan didn't think so. When God asked Satan to "consider my servant Job" (Job 1:8), Satan's immediate response was, "Does Job fear God for nothing?" (Job 1:9).

Ah, the enemy knew. He had watched, up until that

point, the faithfulness and goodness God had poured into Job's life. Satan understood God's character had become so real, so tangible to Job, that even his power—the enemy's power—couldn't be victorious over it. No temptation, no trick, and no whisper of doubt could break the loyalty of someone who had consistently experienced the faithfulness of God's provision. That kind of history with the Lord was too powerful—even for Satan.

Earlier in Job's life, before he had walked so long with God, Satan might've jumped at the chance to test him. But now? Now Job had built something with God. He had been supported time and time again by God's impeccable character. At that point the enemy probably realized this might be a waste of his time.

You see a similar faith in the story of the three Hebrew boys in Daniel chapter 3: Shadrach, Meshach, and Abednego. They were commanded to bow down to the golden image King Nebuchadnezzar had built, and they refused—not once but twice. With the furnace of fire looming, their answer was as bold as it gets:

> If it be so, our God whom we serve is able to deliver us from the furnace of blazing fire, and He will deliver us out of your hand, O King. But even if He does not, let it be known to you, O king, that we are not going to serve your gods or worship the golden image that you have set up.
> —DANIEL 3:17–18

Even if God doesn't deliver us from the fire, we won't bow. Those young men knew what Job knew. That morning I realized I knew it too.

Shadrach, Meshach, and Abednego had experienced

God's character for so long that they understood: Whatever happens, God was still good. So they spoke it aloud for all to hear. *Even if* God doesn't deliver us—*even if* we are thrown into this furnace—we won't bow to anything else. We'll still trust Him. That is the kind of strong bond God builds within His faithful ones.

This brings me to the second part of Job's declaration: "Though He slay me, I will hope in Him" (Job 13:15). Other versions translate it, "Yet I will trust Him."

This sentence has ministered to me deeply. When I wrote this chapter, I began praying over the verse, and the Lord gave me insight. He pointed out that Job was trusting in what he had experienced about God. This wasn't a flippant "I trust in God" cliché we mutter when we're terrified and trying to convince ourselves we're OK. This was a calculated declaration, one carrying the weight of Job's entire life—a life rich with experiences always met by God's character and His faithfulness. It was a *shout of victory* against Satan himself, saying, "*Even if* God takes my life, I know Him too well not to trust His hand."

Job wasn't merely trusting in the *name* of God—though that alone would've been enough. It was deeper. He was trusting in the character traits the name itself represents. Job was proclaiming his allegiance to the name of God because of the character of God.

Now, there is no way I could give you a comprehensive list of every attribute of our mighty God. There are simply too many incredible facets. The thought alone gives me anxiety. (Ha!) But if you'll allow me, I'd like to highlight five of God's incredible characteristics—truths that Job and I both clung to when we couldn't hear His voice for ourselves. These are iron-clad truths you can stand on when God is silent.

1. God is omnipotent—He is all-powerful

"Ah Lord GOD! Behold, You have made the heavens and the earth by Your great power and by Your outstretched arm! Nothing is too difficult for You" (Jer. 32:17). This trait was undoubtedly displayed to Job as he watched the birth of his cattle and flocks. He saw the miracle that no human effort could produce. The hand of the Almighty was obvious. God brings things to being. God blesses and creates. God's power is unmatched.

2. God is faithful

"The steadfast love of the LORD never ceases; His mercies never come to an end; they are new every morning; great is your faithfulness" (Lam. 3:22–23, ESV). Job knew this one well. His wealth multiplied. His livestock reproduced, season after season. God faithfulness to him was cyclical—it never ran dry. It became something Job could count on, even in the face of utter tragedy.

3. God is holy—He is perfect

"You shall be holy, for I the LORD your God am holy" (Lev. 19:2). Job believed this. As previously mentioned, every week he made sacrifices on behalf of his sons—just in case—to ensure that they were forgiven for any sin they might've committed. He didn't treat God's holiness lightly; Job honored it.

4. God is generous—He provides

"If you then, being evil, know how to give good gifts to your children, how much more will your Father who is in heaven give what is good to those who ask Him" (Matt. 7:11). Job experienced provision on a scale that only God could orchestrate. The amount of wealth he acquired was so vast he knew God had provided it. The provision of God has often shocked me. After building businesses, ministries, and a family for so many decades, I've watched God come through repeatedly. He always provides. His generosity never runs out, nor does His provision. Whatever you need—help, money, wisdom, or a fresh perspective—the Lord continually gives. His generosity doesn't expire. Job knew that.

5. God is our refuge and our help

"He who dwells in the shelter of the Most High will abide in the shadow of the Almighty. I will say to the Lord, 'My refuge and fortress, My God in whom I trust'" (Ps. 91:1–2). Given Job's situation, this may seem contradictory, but I believe Job still saw God as his fortress and could trust in His protection. Think about it—his wife had given birth to ten children, and she survived every single one. Job witnessed the protection of the Lord again and again. Until the day of testing, he had lived a life surrounded by divine refuge. As we will see in a later chapter, even during his distress, God's protection didn't disappear.

This list only begins to describe God's character traits. But when you experience even *one*, you can taste and see the goodness of the Lord. Job had experienced these and then some. Because of God's character, Job could confidently say, "Though He slay me, I will hope in Him" (Job 13:15).

God also knew what He had shown Job. He knew He had educated Job for this moment. God had prepared him for this season of silence. He knew the many facets of His character Job had encountered, and He knew what had grown in Job as a result: faith. God had measured Job's faith—He saw its depth. He saw just how much weight it could bear without breaking because Job had walked with Him long enough to witness His power, provision, and presence over and over again.

God didn't offer just *anyone* for Satan to test; He chose the one whose faith would stand the test. God knew Job's faith. He knew, based on their relationship, that Job could withstand the weight of the horrific trials ahead. Job's faith was sturdy, and God knew just how sturdy. God didn't allow one weight too many—nothing that would tip the scales in Satan's favor. He only allowed what Job's faith could triumph over.

God knew Job would never hand over his faith to the enemy. He knew Job would respond with those unforgettable words: "Though He slay me, yet will I hope in Him." Job's faith was never up for grabs. It was secure—fortified by decades of experiencing God's unchanging character. So when Job said, "yet I will trust in Him," he wasn't just referring to God's name, presence, or even His word; Job trusted unequivocally in God's character.

OK, now let's focus on you and where you're at.

I sense that you're struggling. Whatever you're walking through, know that right this second, I'm praying for you. I'm asking the Lord to give me the words that your desperate heart is longing for.

Let me start with this statement: What you are facing is *hard*. Maybe, like me, you're looking at the complete destruction of many things you once relied on. Perhaps your anxiety feels out of control. Perhaps what has worked before in your relationship with God—hearing His voice and experiencing His presence—just isn't working this time. You can't feel Him. You can't find Him. Even the pages of Scripture seem silent, and that silence feels dangerous. Like a harmful bacteria left to grow in the dark, unhealthy thoughts and questions begin to multiply.

No matter how long you've walked with the Lord, look at Job. Even the most faithful among us experience seasons of silence that shake us to our core. We wrestle with questions we're afraid to ask. There are times when the silence is deafening, and our questions seem almost disrespectful. But hear me: Don't pull away. Don't suppress the questions. Don't shrink back from your frustration. Be bold. Bring your questions before the Lord and ask them.

If the answers don't come on your timetable, order your mind back to His character. Recall who He's been to you. Stir up those stories. Fan the flame. It's time to wake the lion inside you.

Take a minute and order your mind to remember how the character of God has led you your entire life. Perhaps you have experienced a miraculous healing. Meditate on the attribute of His character that moved with compassion to heal you. Have you witnessed a financial miracle? Remember what it felt like when His provision met your desperate circumstance.

He hasn't changed. One of His character traits is that He doesn't change. "For I, the LORD, do not change" (Mal. 3:6). The same God who came through for you before will come through again. His character forbids Him to forsake you. "Never will I leave you; never will I forsake you" (Heb. 13:5, NIV).

As that spring morning stretched into the afternoon, I was so moved by the sermon the trees had preached to me about God's character, I decided to buy a weeping willow tree and plant it in my backyard. I wanted a visible reminder for years to come that God's faithfulness *did* eventually come through in that hard season of my life.

Here's a funny story: I'm not a minimalist, so I bought three willow trees that day. Why not, right? Your girl loves trees. Today those once-tiny saplings have grown into large, graceful trees that shade our backyard. Not long after I planted them, the Lord began speaking loudly to my anxiety.

He calmed it. He met me, and I experienced Him in such a way that it changed me forever.

I needed the silence. That quiet was my invitation to lean in and listen to His whisper. I will never forget what He said.

I will leave you a portion of a Psalm that the Lord instructed me to close this chapter on His character with. This happens to be the first verse after the Book of Job concludes. It captures what it looks like to be rooted in God's character—like those trees in my yard, grounded and growing.

> How blessed is the man who does not walk in the counsel of the wicked, nor stand in the path of sinners, nor sit in the seat of scoffers! But his delight is in the law of the LORD, and in his law he meditates day and night. He will be like a tree firmly planted by streams of water, which yield its fruit in its season and its leaf does not wither; and in whatever he does, he prospers.
>
> —PSALM 1:1–4

Scan this QR code or visit AutumnMilesBooks.com/holyghosted/resources to watch a brief video from me with encouragement and deeper insight for your journey.

Chapter 4
HOLY WORD—THE WORD OF GOD THAT SUSTAINS US

*Heaven and earth will pass away, but
My words will not pass away.*
—Matthew 24:35

THE PLANE PLUMMETED several feet—for what was long enough to cause me real concern. As a seasoned flier, I could feel the aircraft losing altitude. This wasn't just turbulence. I waited for an update from the pilot, but none came. Just as suddenly as we had dropped, the plane thrusted upward again, jolting my body with it. I gripped the seat back in front of me, bracing myself for the unknown.

It was a late evening flight back to Indiana, where I lived at the time, after a long week of speaking. I was weary, and for several weeks I had felt extremely unwell. My entire body ached, and I was overcome by a kind of exhaustion that wasn't normal for me. I could barely sit up and have a conversation without needing to lie down soon afterward. My body was even shaking at times—something I had never experienced before. Just waking up was a chore, not to mention showering and getting ready for the day. The physical symptoms had me concerned. I hadn't told anyone—not even Eddie—because, to be honest, I believed something could be seriously wrong.

I stared at the back of the seat in front of me, watching my own fingers cling to the headrest. Luckily, due to the late hour, the plane was barely half full. It was a smaller aircraft, and that night the emptiness felt eerie. Suddenly, the plane plunged again, pulling my attention away from my own white knuckles. I reminded myself that planes can handle all sorts of turbulence—that there was nothing to worry about. But as soon as I comforted myself, we shot upward like a rocket.

This time I closed my eyes.

In all my years of traveling, I had never experienced anything like it. Flying solo most of the time, I've learned to spot people who fear flying. When turbulence hits, they usually stare forward blankly. If traveling with a partner, they'll immediately reach for their hand. Others lean their heads on the seat in front of them, bracing for whatever's coming. If I sense someone nearby is anxious or afraid, I usually try to reassure them and let them know that everything's OK. But that night *I* was the one who was worried.

After about thirty minutes of bouncing up, down, and sideways, the passengers around me began to show their concern. Still no word from the pilot—just the rattle of the cabin and the overhead luggage shifting back and forth with each jolt. I was starting to feel nauseous. A few passengers reached for their handy little motion sickness bags. With my head leaning forward against the seat in front of me, I briefly pulled back to glance around and gauge the emotional temperature of the cabin.

When I did, my eyes locked with a woman sitting in the row ahead. She had turned around and was looking straight at me—not with panic but with quiet pleading, as if I might offer her some comfort. She was the kind of person I would normally reassure—one who clearly had severe flying anxiety. My eyes met hers, and I smiled as if to say, "We're going to make it." However, I wasn't so sure.

As soon as I gave her that smile, the plane took a dive downward again—so sharply that I wondered whether I should brace for impact. I began to pray, "Jesus, save us." Truthfully, between my exhaustion, the nausea from the flight, and my fear, I had no other words. I kept waiting for the pilot to come over the intercom to calm our nerves, but only silence filled the air. All we could hear—or feel—was the chaos around us. Terror was thick in the cabin.

I kept praying the same phrase, "Jesus, save us."

In the middle of the most horrendous flight I've ever taken, the Lord spoke to me, loudly and authoritatively. He said, "Autumn, do not fear; you are pregnant with a baby girl." Stunned, I sat as still as possible to see whether He would say it again. Then I heard it again, clear as day: "Autumn, do not fear; you are pregnant with a baby girl."

This wasn't one of those moments where I needed time to discern or meditate on what I heard. I knew—not because of a pregnancy test, not because of symptoms, but because I had just heard the word of the Lord, and I *knew* it was true. A supernatural peace filled my spirit. It was something that I couldn't explain in words. The plane was still bouncing around the empty night sky, but I was suddenly unbothered.

Not only did God Himself just tell me I was pregnant, but He also confirmed that I didn't need to fear what was happening, because I *would* give birth to a baby girl. God had given me a sure word—one that calmed my fear, carried me through the rest of that terrifying flight, and held me steady when everything else felt unstable. It was the word I needed to remain calm amid what seemed to be impending doom. I chose to trust *that* word over the violent tossing of the aircraft.

I trusted that God had an incredible future ahead for me and Eddie, and that I didn't need be afraid. I trusted that the baby girl I would name Grace—the one I had boldly asked God to bless me with after the divorce from my first husband—was finally on her way. What about the sickness I had been experiencing? It wasn't something to fear. I was pregnant. God had spoken.

The flight actually got worse before it got better. Even through the roughest turbulence, I kept meditating on the word God had given me rather than my circumstances:

"Autumn, do not fear; you are pregnant with a baby girl."

God's Word calmed me in a way nothing else could. It *was* peace.

THE ONLY WORD THAT MATTERS IN A CRISIS

I share the story you just read as an example of God's word sustaining me in a crisis, but the truth is, I have hundreds of similar stories just like that. The Holy Spirit spoke directly to me that night, but He has spoken to me through the Bible thousands of other times. Whether from the Holy Spirit or the Bible, this one thing is true: It won't fail.

Grace, my firstborn daughter, was born eight and a half months later on October 9, 2005. Just as Gabriel told Mary she would bear the Christ Child, God Himself told me I would have a baby girl—no pregnancy test needed. God gave me a word, and He saw it through to completion. No force on earth or beneath it can override the word of God. It is impossible for His word not to yield the exact reason that it is sent (Isa. 55:11).

No hardship, no number of trials, not even the threat of death is more powerful than the Word of God. In Genesis we see God's Word creating the world, and the things He created with words in Genesis are still alive today. He created them with seeds within them to sustain them (v. 1). His word is that powerful.

His Word retains its potency through the passage of time, through circumstances that seem to contradict it, and even through our moments of wavering faith. His Word will still stand, even when we cannot. Even a season of silence from Him doesn't stop the promises He has already given. Nothing can stop it.

In chapter 3 we focused on standing on the character of God in a season of silence from God, especially when it is coupled with heavy trials. But the other sustaining pillar we need to stand on is God's Word. What has He told you? What verses have built your life? What promises do you stand on? In a season when God seems silent, remember what He *has* said. Stand on those words. Those words will comfort and sustain you. We live our lives based on His Word and between His words. So when you don't have a fresh word about your current situation, remember a past word from God that has sustained you.

Crisis bows to the Word of God.

Kings bow to the Word of God, often without even knowing they are doing so.

Creation submits to it.

Bad theology can't stop it.

If He gives it, it can't be stopped by anything.

Job knew this truth. As devastated as Job was, he clung to the word of God. Though the text doesn't give us much of a backstory on Job's personal relationship with God before tragedy struck, we do see him standing on the word of God in the aftermath of losing it all. This tells us that Job had to rely on His word in times of lesser struggles, and in those seasons God performed what He had spoken. This built Job's dependence on God's word.

Job's reliance on God's word sustained his faith during the silence. Job declares to his friends this staggering hope: "But it is still my consolation, and I rejoice in the unsparing pain, that I have not denied the words of the Holy One" (Job 6:10).

We don't know what words Job was referring to, yet he was clearly depending on the word of God to carry him. He knew that denying God's word—or running from it—would mean running from the hope it brings. He knew that the word would still stand long after his season of horror was over.

He knew what David knew when he penned: "This God— his way is perfect; the word of the LORD proves true; he is a shield for all those who take refuge in him" (Ps. 18:30, ESV).

David, Job, and I all knew this one thing: The word of God is to be trusted more than anything you face—it will prove to be true.

ACTIVATE THE POWER OF THE WORD OF GOD

This is something that I had to learn the hard way. I didn't know how to activate the power of the Word of God alone. Don't get me wrong. I grew up a Baptist girl, so I knew what was in the Word of God. But knowing what's in the Bible and activating its power are two entirely different things.

Knowing the contents of the Bible and applying them to your life are not the same. I fear this is how Satan has confused so many who walk away from the faith; they recognize the Bible but have never activated its power. Satan knows the Word of God and knows how powerful it is, and he absolutely doesn't want you to use it.

But friend, knowing what the Word of God says is not enough. If you stop there, the Bible will eventually become just another historical document—one you'll eventually find irrelevant when life gets hard. However, when adversity or spiritual trials hit, that is the *best* time to activate the Word of God in your life and watch it prove itself to be true.

God doesn't want you to break. He doesn't want you to give up. He doesn't want you to stop believing because your circumstances are crushing. He wants you to believe His Word and activate its power in your life. He knows His Word is hope. He knows the power it holds, and He wants that power active in your life.

The wisdom of Agur in Proverbs echoes the same truth David wrote in the Psalms: "Every word of God proves true; he is a shield to those who take refuge in him" (Prov. 30:5, ESV).

This should tell you that if *two* writers from historical biblical books of wisdom declare that God's Word will prove true—it will. Circumstances don't matter. God's Word is more powerful.

OK, I know you are wondering, "How in this world do I activate it?"

I'm glad you asked, friend.

Here is what the Bible says about itself: "For the word of God is living and active and sharper than any two-edged sword, and piercing as far as the division of soul and spirit, of both joints and marrow, and able to judge the thoughts and intentions of the heart" (Heb. 4:12).

If the Word of God is truly living, alive, and active, should we read it as simply a historical document? Or should we use it as the living, breathing truth that it is?

Another way of saying it is, the Word of God longs to be alive and active in your life. But, you, my sweet friend, who I am desperately trying to speak to, have to do the faith work of activation. The good news is, it's easier than you think.

I want you to begin by reading the Bible differently. Read it as truth. Read it as relevant for you *right now*—whatever situation you find yourself in. Look at every word as a counselor. When you read the Word of God as fact and approach it as a counselor, it shifts from being mere historical information to becoming essential—something you can't live without.

Now couple that active reading with this fact: God's Word has the power to do exactly what it says. What Scripture promises, it performs. If the promise is peace, it has the power to deliver peace. If the promise is deliverance, it has the power to deliver. If the promise is direction, God's Word will guide you.

The following are three things to remember when you activate Scripture:

1. Scripture is truth.

2. Scripture is my counselor.

3. Scripture is equipped with the power it claims to have.

The truth found in the Word of God is substance. You can count on it, as it offers the only words we can truly stand on. Even when the turbulence of that flight made me feel like the plane might crash, when the word of God spoke to me, it became the ground beneath me—something more real than what I was feeling.

As a truth-teller myself, I have to say this: God's Word is truer than I am on my most truthful day. I can only speak from my limited perspective, but the Word of God sees the end from the beginning. It pierces between soul and spirit. It judges not just actions but the intentions of the heart. How on earth could I do that? I can't, but the Word of God can. God's Word is a truer truth than anything else that is true.

So now, when you face any single one of the horrific trials that Job endured, you can cling to Scripture the way Job did. He knew that God's words were truer than true and that His counsel was powerful. That's why he clung to them. Let me show you what he said in Job 6:10, "But it is still my consolation, and I rejoice in unsparing pain, that I have not denied the words of the Holy One." He stood on God's Word when everything else gave way. He focused on it—it took all his attention because he knew it would prove to be true eventually. He activated it; it became his bread—his survival at that time. He had nothing else but the word of God, and he knew it was all he needed to get him to the other side.

Here's a fascinating historical fact: Many scholars believe the Book of Job is the oldest in the Bible—older even than the Torah.[1] The Torah (Genesis, Exodus, Leviticus, Numbers, and Deuteronomy) was probably compiled in written form between 450 and 350 BC, but Job may have been written before that time period. In those days the Word of God was passed down orally—from person to person, generation to generation—before it was written down. This means Job may have been referring to the oral transmission of the Word of God, unless he had an encounter we don't know about (which is entirely possible).

OK, that was a lot—sorry. But here's the point: The Word of God was so powerful to Job that even spoken words, passed down from someone else, were worth staking his hope on. He knew the strength of God's very words—that they were true, that they were his counselor, and that they held power. This was enough for him to stand on, even during his journey of severe grief and depression.

Romans 10:17 says, "So then faith comes by hearing, and hearing by the word of God" (NKJV).

Job *literally heard* the Word of God, and the faith deposited in his heart because of what he heard from God grew. Isn't that amazing? What a miracle.

This one makes me weep.

We always have the entire Word of God in front of us. It's there for us to open and read anytime we like. Since Pentecost, we also have access to the Spirit of God, who speaks to us, helps us, comforts us, and guides us. Yet we so often ignore these luxuries and forsake the power that the living Word of God offers.

But Job preaches to us. He challenges us to do better. He calls us to take God at His word.

Because even if it was orally transmitted, the Word of God was the truest truth for Job.

THE WORD OF THE LORD TRIED HIM

While the Word of God can, without question, be trusted because it is true, there are seasons of intense trial when that very truth is hard to hold on to. We can read it as truth, as counsel, as power, and still find ourselves struggling to believe it. Before we wrap up this chapter, I want to talk to you about how sometimes believing God's Word becomes even more difficult than enduring the trial itself.

During deepest suffering—the loss of a child, a health crisis, or something equally crushing—hope becomes the real trial. We mock hope. We mock in laughter the thought of restoration. We grow cynical about the deliverance God's Word promises. And if we aren't careful, we give up on activating the Word of God because the test of our faith feels more extreme than the hardship.

Sarah mocked God. Remember Sarah, Abraham's wife? God promised Abraham a son—an heir to the covenant, the beginning of a lineage that would make him "the father of many nations" (Gen. 17:5, NIV). But the word of the Lord tested them. I dare say it tested them more than their physical inability to conceive. The idea that they would conceive became harder to believe than simply accepting that they couldn't.

Sometimes giving up seems easier than believing the victory is still coming. Accepting the terminal diagnosis can feel easier than fighting for healing. I get that—so does God. I've lived that tension. Perhaps you're living it right now. Is believing the Word of the Lord harder for you in this moment than simply accepting defeat? If so, this section is for you.

When God finally came to Abraham and Sarah and told them that, by this time next year, Sarah would have a son, she laughed (Gen. 18:10–14). She didn't laugh out of joy—she laughed in disbelief, in mockery: "She laughed to herself, saying, 'After I have become old, am I to have pleasure, my lord being old also?'" (Gen. 18:12).

The Hebrew word for *laugh* in this passage, *tsachaq*, can also mean "mockery or scorn."[2] Sarah mocked the word of the Lord because, by this point, it felt easier to trust the limitations of her body than to trust the word of God.

God often uses His word to try us and test us. Believing His word becomes the test—not just accepting "what is." This happened to Joseph too. As a young boy, Joseph had a dream—God's Word revealed to him that his brothers would one day bow down to him (Gen. 37:5–11). But soon after he shared this dream with his family, his life looked nothing like it. His brothers betrayed him, sold him into slavery, and told their father that he was dead (Gen. 37:12–36). He became a servant in Potiphar's house, only to be falsely accused by Potiphar's wife, which landed him in prison (Gen. 39:1–20).

The Bible tells us in the Psalms that, when Joseph was in prison, the "word of the Lord tried him." Let's read the passage: "He sent a man before them, Joseph, who was sold as a slave. They afflicted his feet with fetters, he himself was laid in irons; until the time that his word came to pass, the word of the LORD tested him" (Ps. 105:17–19).

What does this mean? Well, God had given Joseph a dream—a sure word from Himself. But the reality of sitting in a prison cell looked nothing like his brothers bowing down to him. In fact, it directly contradicted the dream. That's why Scripture says the word of the Lord tested him. The word of the Lord pushed against every fiber of his faith. Believing what God said was harder than accepting what he saw. The word of God tried him more than his circumstances did.

God's word tried Moses at the Red Sea (Exodus 14). It tried Joshua at the battle of Jericho (Joshua 6). It tried Jesus in Gethsemane (Matthew 26, Mark 14, Luke 22, John 18). And it tried our friend Job too.

Job declared, "My foot has held fast to His path; I have kept His way and not turned aside. I have not departed the command of His lips; I have treasured the words of His mouth more than my necessary food" (Job 23:11–12).

Even in a season of drastic loss and silence from heaven, Job didn't turn aside. He didn't forsake the word of the Lord or surrender to defeat. Though the word of God tried him, he wouldn't waver. He knew it would stand in the end.

WHERE ARE YOU?

I wrote this chapter on the Word of God as an answer to the question: "What do I do in a season of harsh trials when God is silent?" The first option is located in chapter 3—to rely on what you know about God's character. The second option is in this chapter—to rely on the Word of God.

I wrote this book for those who are being crushed in their spirit, who see no way forward, whose questions are many, and whose faith is slipping. I don't want this book to waste your time. I want it to be an answer—a resource for what your heart is truly craving: hope.

So I speak to you as your favorite aunt who brings the best chocolate chip cookies to every family gathering, sitting beside you at the Christmas dinner table, saying, "You will come through this. There is life on the other side of this. I know what you are facing feels like it's breaking you, but it is not stronger than the Word of God that will restore you. Your trial is not stronger than the power of God to redeem it. Don't you dare give up on His Word and settle for defeat. We don't do that in this family. We rise. So rise up. Stomp your feet on the Word of God and stand on its substance. Nothing is stronger than the God inside you. I'm here to help. Don't let Satan have this win. Let's give him a defeat."

I gave birth to Grace Miles on a beautiful Sunday morning in October 2005. Do you want to know the funny thing about that terrifying plane ride? It became a metaphor for my pregnancy with Grace. For the first five months of my pregnancy, I was bedridden—so severely ill that I was hospitalized with severe dehydration. My body was pulling fluids from my organs just to keep her alive. I didn't realize it at the time, but I had a medical condition—one my own mother had also suffered during her pregnancy. Eddie and

I couldn't afford the medication to treat the symptoms. As a result, I was sicker than I had ever been. When I arrived at the hospital to deliver Grace, I had lost twenty pounds. During labor, we both were in distress, and the team prepared an emergency C-section with the cart ready to wheel me into surgery. Suddenly, we didn't need it. God moved in my body, and I delivered the word God had given me that day on the plane: a baby girl.

I needed that word God gave me on the plane. God knew what I was about to face in my pregnancy. I needed something to cling to through every wave of nausea and every quiet moment of fear. I needed to know that, no matter what my circumstances looked like, I had something more solid than the symptoms—a sure word from God—and He did it.

She came in like a hurricane and has been the manifestation of God's grace in my life ever since. Her name is what she is to me: Grace.

I don't know what you are facing but hold fast. Job 23:10 says, "But He knows the way I take; when He has tried me, I shall come forth as gold." Just as Job was confident that God was watching and intimately aware of his circumstances, God is present in yours. He knows what's happening in your life right now that has you on the verge of giving in.

Trust me: When I was so sick with Grace that I couldn't lift my head, and when I was too weak even to read the Bible, I knew the Lord was watching over me. God was silent to me in that season, but the word He gave before the trial was *loud*. My body was attacking itself, but the word of the Lord would not let me completely succumb to it. My mind was full of doubts about His goodness, but His word screamed louder. Just like Job, I came forth as gold. So did my daughter.

Friend, you will too. His Word is the truest truth. Activate it. It will prove faithful no matter what your circumstances are shouting. They are lying to you. His Word will accomplish what He sent it to do—to bring you hope.

Scan this QR code or visit AutumnMilesBooks.com/holyghosted/resources to watch a brief video from me with encouragement and deeper insight for your journey.

Chapter 5
UNHOLY ASSUMPTIONS—DON'T ASSUME THINGS ABOUT GOD

*If one gives an answer before he
hears, it is his folly and shame.*
—PROVERBS 18:13, ESV

G OD WANTS ME dead. He wants to kill me. He is
going to kill me," I thought, as I drove my black
Jeep Cherokee to work before sunrise around 4:30
a.m. My hands began to shake at the thought. The tremors
had become routine—my body's rebellion against relentless chronic stress. I dropped my left, shaky hand down to
engage the turn signal. Sitting at a four-way stop, I looked
both ways to check for traffic. When I didn't see another
car through the darkness, I looked again—still nothing. At
that point I questioned everything and didn't trust my own
eyes, so I checked a third time. I saw nothing. Finally, my
trembling right foot found the courage to press the gas. As
I slowly took my turn, I silently breathed a sigh of relief. I
hadn't imagined it; the road truly was clear.

"You better be thankful that a car didn't come out of
nowhere and kill you. After all, God is after you," I thought.
My heart began to race, as my mind taunted me with the

idea it was only a matter of time before God would strike me down.

I hadn't slept much the night before. I had gotten into the habit of watching all the late-night shows on TV to stay awake. I was convinced that if I fell asleep, God would take me in the night. But if I stayed awake, I would rob Him of the opportunity. That meant He'd have to find another way—maybe in the car on the way to work.

I had daydreamed about how it might happen. Would it be an accident? A murder? A hit-and-run? The scenarios were endless. God could do it any way He wanted, and there was nothing I could do about it. While I didn't know which method He would choose, it didn't matter. All I knew was that it would happen. I was bracing for it. I had convinced myself that God hated me and wanted me dead.

The thought that God would kill me was one I had nursed for quite some time. I'm not sure when it started, but I knew I had made a lot of mistakes. I had sinned so many times. According to the theology I grew up with—a God of wrath and judgment—my days were numbered. I was certain He was angry with me and wanted to punish me with the ultimate consequence: death.

I looked at what had become of my life with disgust. I was trapped in a terrible marriage. I hated every single day. I hated my life. I dreaded waking up and facing the dark, morbid thoughts that looped endlessly in my mind. I was twenty years old, working three jobs, and trying to survive the abuse I was experiencing at home. Somewhere along the way, I had absorbed the fear-based theology from my childhood. "God is a God of wrath and judgment," I would remind myself regularly. "God will judge you for all the things you have done wrong," I also often remembered this one: "God is a just God, and if you don't fall in line with what He tells you, He may take your life." Yes, those were my dark, hourly thoughts.

Let me take a break from this depressing story to tell you something: I like flowers—especially happy yellow ones. They are sunny, beautiful, and just so happen to be my favorite color. I also like Diet Coke and hot fudge. Fun fact: When I was pregnant with Grace, I went to an ice cream shop, ordered a bowl of hot fudge, and ate the whole thing. It was the best thing I've ever eaten. OK, let's continue. I felt like it was getting a little too dark.

As these assumptions about God became the dominant narrative in my head, I felt compelled not to tell a soul about them. I was ashamed, completely embarrassed by my own thoughts. I wondered, "Who thinks like this on a daily basis?" I mean, what would my preacher daddy think if he knew his daughter believed that God would kill her at any moment? What would my preacher's wife—my mom—say if I told her that I was convinced God hated me? Would my Sunday school teacher quit if I shared that their fear-based theology had buried itself so deep? Did I truly believe that God was after me to cause me harm? Yes, I did.

Yes, I was still faithfully attending church this entire time. Who could I tell—my brother and sister? My brother played guitar for the university's worship band, and my sister had just rededicated her life to Christ. Nope, I saw them as the righteous ones. I assumed they would judge me too. I was sure they wouldn't understand, so I decided it was best to stay silent. It didn't matter anyway; I didn't think I was long for this world. After all, death was imminent in my mind.

That morning I drove the speed limit to the restaurant where I waited tables, moving with the utmost caution. It was a small personal victory just to drive more than five miles from home. I had decided anything beyond five miles was too dangerous.

Before I arrived, I clicked my turn signal again at a stoplight. This time my eyes locked on the neon lights of the gas station. I stared blankly. My mind-numbing stare gave me a momentary break from the storm in my mind. It was the pause I needed.

When the light turned green, something inside me shifted too. Sitting alone in my car under the early morning sky, I broke.

My tears came violently. My body was already shaking with anxiety and fear, and now it shook from months of pent-up sobbing. I pulled into the empty parking lot of the restaurant and sobbed. My tears wouldn't stop.

I knew I had to ring the doorbell to open the store at 4:45 a.m., but the clock read 4:52 a.m. I was trying to stop the flood of emotion before going inside, but my body wouldn't cooperate. I was late and didn't know how to explain it. "I'm crying because I'm scared God is going to kill me"—can you imagine saying that to your boss? No, he would think I was some sort of psycho.

At 4:55 a.m. I had no choice. I grabbed my apron, opened the car door, and walked to the entrance still sobbing. My manager stood waiting, arms crossed. He looked stern at first, but as I approached, I saw the concern in his eyes. He could see everything: the emotion, the pain.

He had never seen me like this before. I was usually the happy employee, cracking jokes and looking at the positive side of life. I stopped at the door and waited while he unlocked it. He said only one thing: "Go get cleaned up, Autumn, and take all the time you need."

I walked straight to the restroom and hid in a stall. Several minutes later, I managed to compose myself enough to enter the kitchen, where he greeted me with a warm, "Would you like to talk in my office?" Without answering, I walked in and sat silently for several minutes. He sat across from me and said nothing. There was no pressure for me to speak—just a sense of compassion and support.

My face and eyes were puffy and swollen from the afore-mentioned episode. I apologized for my appearance and for my tardiness. He responded with compassion, saying something like, "This too shall pass." Though it was a cliché, it was what I needed to move forward that day.

We sat in silence for at least twenty minutes. He didn't say anything else. There was no judgment or anger. There was only peace. Though he wasn't even a believer, his calming presence ministered to me that morning.

Isn't it funny how God will sometimes use people who don't even know Him to be a messenger of hope? That day my manager was a godsend, and he didn't even realize it.

My assumptions about God during that season—along with many other factors—led me into a depression so deep that I couldn't climb out of it. Those lies felt like facts. To me, they were facts. I believed them as truth. Without divine intervention, I would've either renounced my faith or taken my own life just to beat God to it.

QUESTIONS AREN'T THE PROBLEM; ASSUMPTIONS ABOUT GOD ARE

My assumptions about God weren't based on facts from the Word of God; they were based on how I was feeling about God. I didn't hold my assumptions accountable under the authority of Scripture; instead, I relied on my own reasoning. I had many questions about God: for instance, why would He allow me to go through such an awful relationship and not intervene?

The questions I had about God weren't the problem. Until the end of time, mankind will wrestle with the decisions God makes and the situations He allows in our lives. God can handle the questions because He can answer them all. He has an answer for every question you could ever dream of asking, and quite frankly He would love to engage with you on a more intimate level to help you understand.

He is generous with His communication when we are ready to receive it. In the following chapters, I will argue that your questions about your situation shouldn't be dismissed but explored fully. However, in this chapter I want to caution you about the assumptions our human minds often attach to those questions.

For example, I questioned whether God cared about what I was going through in my first marriage. But with that question came an assumption: He didn't care because He hadn't intervened yet. Whether He cared wasn't the problem; my assumption that He didn't was. That assumption was a lie. God did care, but I lived under the weight of the lie, and it separated me from hope. He was my only hope, but my assumptions hindered me from seeing the truth. As a result, I saw God as the enemy.

THE ASSUMPTION TRAP IN JOB'S STORY

Assumptions are one of Job's biggest hidden themes. Job assumed lies about God. His friends assumed lies about Job and God. What about Satan? He assumed lies about Job. Whew, that was a mouthful. I don't want to confuse you, so let's start with Job and his assumptions about God.

With many of Job's natural questions, he attached

assumptions. In Job 9:24, during his suffering, he asks, "If it is not He, then who is it?" This is a legitimate question. He's wondering whether it was God who caused all his pain. To me, this seems like a reasonable question, as there is no violation in asking. The problem lies in the declarations Job made leading up to it, where he assumes God is the culprit. Let's get into it:

> For He bruises me with a tempest and multiplies my wounds without cause. He will not allow me to get my breath, but saturates me with bitterness.... He destroys the guiltless and the wicked. If the scourge kills suddenly, He mocks the despair of the innocent. The earth is given into the hands of the wicked; He covers the faces of its judges.
> —Job 9:17–18, 22–24

Before you judge Job, remember what he's going through: He's in deep grief and depression. But look at what he begins to assume about God:

- "He bruises me" (v. 17).
- "He will not allow me to catch my breath" (v. 18).
- "He destroys the guiltless" (v. 22).
- "He mocks the despair of the innocent" (v. 23).

Wow, look at these assumptions about God. They may have started as feelings, but Job spoke them as declarations. He assumed they were true.

For instance, Job assumed that God was causing all the destruction in his life. He believed the hand of the Lord had brought it, but Job 1:12–19 and Job 2:7 tell us the opposite:

The hand of Satan was responsible for the terror he was feeling, not the hand of God.

God had done none of it, yet Job assumed He did.

Do you see how problematic it was for Job to assume that God was responsible for his terror? God received the blame for something He didn't even do—as is often the case. God often is blamed for things He is not guilty of.

BE HONEST: HAVE YOU EVER BLAMED GOD?

Have you ever blamed God for doing something He didn't do? Or assumed God was responsible for the hard times in your life? We need to sit on this for a minute.

People have long assumed that God was responsible for things He didn't do. God's hand didn't destroy Job's life—Satan's did. This account gives us a rare glimpse into the spiritual realm, where Satan roams the earth to see whose life he can destroy. Job 1:7 tells us this plainly: Satan is roaming, seeking someone to harm. First Peter 5:8 echoes the warning: "Be of sober spirit, be on the alert. Your adversary, the devil, prowls around like a roaring lion, seeking someone to devour." John 10:10 makes his mission even clearer: "The thief comes only to steal and kill and destroy."

You may have heard these verses a thousand times, but they're in the Bible for a reason: to help us identify where the real threats come from and place blame where it belongs.

People have left the faith because they've blamed God—for a marriage that failed, the loss of a child, or some other tragedy. Let me say this clearly: These are horrific circumstances. Absolutely horrific. But people have left the church in droves—not because God failed them, but because they assumed He did. They want nothing to do with God because they blame Him for something He didn't do.

My husband once had a conversation with a former pastor, which is seared in my mind. To be honest, I've had many of these conversations over the years too. Through tears this former pastor shared why they gave up ministry altogether. Assuming the worst about God, he blamed Him for the attacks that he experienced in ministry. The pastor believed God was his enemy—not Satan. He stopped going to church and gave up on God entirely.

You've heard this story before, haven't you? "I was once on fire for the Lord, but then..." You can fill in the blank. The trial was so hard that, in their pain, they assumed God wasn't good. Rather than running to the Lord for comfort, some people run away from Him in search of relief.

The following is another example of Job's questions, coupled with an assumption about God: "Why do You hide Your face and consider me Your enemy?" (Job 13:24).

This is a natural human question. We ask questions like these all the time: "God, where are You? Why are You hiding Your face?" Even David asks, in the book that follows Job, Psalms: "How long, O Lord? Will You forget me forever? How long will You hide Your face from me?" (Ps. 13:1).

But notice what David does: He stops with the question.

Job, however, attaches an assumption. He believes that not only is God hiding His face but God considers him an enemy. That assumption couldn't be further from the truth. According to Job 1 and 2, God considered Job one of His greatest allies—not the enemy's.

"Have you considered my servant Job? There is no one on earth like him; he is blameless and upright, a man who fears God and shuns evil. And he still maintains his integrity" (Job 2:3, NIV).

God called Job blameless, upright, and a man of great integrity. Never—not once—did He say Job was His enemy. Yet Job's pain distorted his perception. If we allow it, pain can distort our perception of how good God is. Job assumed God had turned on him, and if we aren't careful, we too can get caught thinking the same thing.

Be careful, friend, about assuming what God thinks about you.

Job was completely wrong. Like, way wrong.

It's hard to live under the belief that God thinks you're His enemy. Trust me—I did just that. Take an audit of your thoughts right now. What do you believe God thinks about you?

If your thoughts don't align with Scripture—with what God has already declared about you—then you need to stop thinking them. That kind of thinking causes deep spiritual damage. It builds false narratives that distance you from hope.

As previously mentioned, dive into what God really thinks about you—not what you think He thinks—especially when life's hard or you're hurting. Seek truth about His thoughts from the pages of His Word, not assumptions based on your feelings.

I admitted to Eddie early in our marriage that I had always believed God was mad at me. It didn't matter what the situation was; I had a hard time accepting that God was truly gracious. Once, I blurted out something like, "I feel like I have to walk on eggshells around God." Eddie paused, looked me in the eye, and said, "That's not God."

That one sentence shifted something in me.

We had a long conversation that day about how I had been raised to fear God—not in the reverent, biblical sense, but in the be-scared-of-God kind of way. It was paralyzing. I had to retrain my mind. I had to learn how to replace my old thoughts and assumptions with the truth about how God truly sees me, not the lie that He was mad at me all the time.

I believe that these false assumptions about God caused Job more harm than the grief he was experiencing, just like they did to me. Job, like many of us, created a barrier between himself and hope—and that's the most dangerous thing we can do in our suffering. Our assumptions about God can create a barrier between us and hope itself.

This is why I intentionally placed chapter 3 (on God's character) and chapter 4 (on God's Word) before this one. We must learn how to process God's silence when a trial hits us hard. If we don't, we'll fall into the same pattern Job did: We'll assume lies. Those lies will steal the very hope we need to survive the storm.

There's so much we can learn from how Job processed his thoughts. The pattern in these verses is deeply instructive. If we'll pay attention, there's great wisdom for us to partake in.

ASSUMPTIONS JOB'S FRIENDS MADE ABOUT GOD LED THEM TO SPEAK FOR HIM

While Job was wrong in assuming what God was doing, his friends—Eliphaz, Bildad, and Zophar (cool names, I know—snag one of them for your next kid)—did something even more cringeworthy. They assumed they knew what God was thinking, but then they took it a step further and began to speak for Him. Their assumption about what God was doing—based on a lack of knowledge about His ways—led to them to incorrectly put words in His mouth. Major no-no.

It's one thing to wrestle silently with what we *think* God might be thinking or doing. But once we start voicing those assumptions with authority—especially when speaking into someone else's life as "truth"—it crosses a dangerous line. When you start judging for God, trying to convince someone they are wrong or sinful based on your perception, you're acting as judge and mouthpiece, and God doesn't like that. He doesn't play around with this.

Job's three friends showed up to comfort Job after he lost everything, which was incredibly admirable. They actually started strong. They traveled to Job, sat beside him in his grief, and perhaps even brought him a nice charcuterie board and some homemade blackberry jam—you know, as you do. The Bible says, "Then they sat down on the ground with him for seven days and seven nights with no one speaking a word to him, for they saw that his pain was very great" (Job 2:13, NIV).

"They saw that his pain was very great." Yeah, you think?

These three guys, while well-meaning, started off in silence—but after the seven days, they just couldn't help themselves. They began to try to "talk some sense" into Job, or what they believed was wisdom. But with such limited understanding of God's ways, their words only picked Job apart.

Most of Job is filled with conversations between him and those friends—discussions about Job's righteousness that reveal more about *their* feeble theology than about Job's actual situation. They were so focused on proving their assumptions about him and about God that they completely missed Job's heart.

This book is fascinating because, as you read their comments, you may start to recognize a few Bildads, Zophars, and Eliphazes in your own life—"friends" who love to tell you everything you are doing wrong in the name of "helping you have a better life." We all know someone who wants to peacock their "great wisdom" in front of us mere "peasants,"

just to appear more righteous than they really are. I know—
harsh, right? Sorry, not sorry. This needs to stop. Instead of
staying compassionate with Job, their tone shifted into full-
blown, self-righteous judgment.

I believe this was another phase in Job's trial where the
enemy was involved. This was a psychological attack on
Job. What did God tell Satan? He said, "Only spare his
life" (Job 2:6). So Job's mind was also up for grabs, and the
doorway to that battlefield was his friends' judgment. The
enemy got into his friends' heads to get into Job's. The con-
demnation was fast and hard. What was their harsh rebuke,
you ask? In their meek view of God, they reasoned that
He would never rebuke a righteous person the way He was
"rebuking" Job, so Job must have unconfessed sin in his life.
They assumed God was angry with Job, and that was why
Job was suffering.

Here it is, straight from their mouths: "Remember, who
that was innocent ever perished? Or where were the upright
cut off? As I have seen, those who plow iniquity and sow
trouble reap the same" (Job 4:7–8, ESV). Let's grab another
"comforting" nugget from one of Job's dearest friends. Bildad
chimes in, saying, "Behold, God will not reject a blameless person, nor take the hand of evildoers" (Job 8:20, ESV).
Eliphaz—another *dear* friend—says,

> Yield now and be at peace with Him; thereby good
> will come to you. Please receive instruction from
> His mouth and establish His words in your heart. If
> you return to the Almighty, you will be restored; if
> you remove unrighteousness far from your tent, and
> place your gold in the dust, and the gold of Ophir
> among the stones of the brooks, then the Almighty

will be your gold and choice silver to you…. You
will pray to Him, and He will hear you.
—Job 22:21–25, 27

These three friends make me want to cry. They assumed,
again and again, that Job must surely be guilty of something—maybe even a hidden sin. In their narrow view of
God, there was just no way a righteous man would suffer
like that. So in their minds, Job needed to repent. But
listen, friend, the truth is that Job was innocent, and God
was *not* mad at him. (See Job 1:1, 1:8, 2:3.) Over and over,
Job tried to tell them this, but they ambushed him with
their self-righteous assumptions, and even he couldn't convince them otherwise. Honestly, I would argue even God
Himself couldn't convince them—their pride was that loud.
The idea was that Job didn't fit their religious narrative or
their self-righteous theology.

They, my sweet friends, were very wrong.

THIS IS SPIRITUAL ABUSE

This is a very clear example of spiritual abuse. His friends
used their understanding of God to try to control and
manipulate Job to repent for something he didn't even do.
They assumed they knew where God stood. They judged
Job incorrectly, spoke for God, and tried to pressure him
into "fixing" something that wasn't even a thing. Yikes, this
is all very bad. Consequently, they got in trouble: At the end
of the book, God Himself told Job that His anger burned
against them (Job 42:7–9).

This should send a shiver down all our spines. We must
be aware that Satan tries to run our churches with this kind
of thing every single day. Yes, I said what I said. Sometimes
Satan himself is trying to shepherd our churches through a

pharisaical, abusive spirit, tempting leaders to assume they know what God is thinking and trying to convince others that they must adhere to those assumptions. Let me say it plainly: Satan will gladly "pastor" us if we let him.

Over the years, many people have told me that I wasn't aligned with God's will for my life. One person said, "If you do this, God will never use you." Another warned, "If you move, it is not God's will for your life." Someone else declared, "I believe God wants you to wait to go into ministry until your children are grown." All the while, I knew for a fact they were wrong—because I was hearing straight from God. This was the enemy trying to get me to listen and halt God's movement in my life. That, friend, is spiritual abuse. In every single situation, God showed up and affirmed that all these voices were wrong—and He did so in very public, often embarrassing ways for those who spoke against me.

Don't even get me started on how many times a preacher or spiritual "leader" has told me that I can't teach God's Word because I'm a woman. Like, countless. When people begin to advise you about what God thinks about you, make sure you know what He really thinks first. Otherwise, the psychological trap the enemy has set may take you out.

In the moment, however, it is hard to hear when people in some sort of authority use God as their source of information to tear you apart. But if you know where you stand with God, you'll be able to see through the scheme. In my life I can declare the truth—not because I asked to be called, but because He wanted me to be a minister of His gospel.

DON'T BE LIKE JOB'S FRIENDS, AND DON'T LISTEN TO THEM

Let me talk to you as a mama for a second, because I love you and I have four kids—so I'm good at it. Don't assume that you know what God thinks about someone unless you know for sure that God Himself has given you a sure word. I never speak on God's behalf to someone else unless I know—beyond a doubt—that He has spoken to me about them. Sometimes I will have a word for someone that I know is from the Lord, but I still wait on His timing before I share it. Here's the deal: Do not share anything and use God's name unless He told you to share it with that person. Absolutely, don't ever use God to manipulate a person or a situation. If you do, He will rebuke you the way He rebuked Job's friends—and trust me, that will be humiliating. God is good at speaking for Himself.

Also, dear ones, don't listen to every person who sounds like they know what they are talking about—even those voices closest to you. Job's friends were close to him but far from the truth about who he was or who God was. That's an important distinction. When someone may be attempting to advise you on your situation, before you receive their instruction, take it to the Lord. Ask God to help you discern whether what they're saying is truly from Him. Ask Him to confirm it through Scripture or by the Holy Spirit.

SO NOW WHAT?

I wrote this chapter because chances are you may have made assumptions about God without even realizing it. It might sound something like this: "God doesn't hear my prayer. I've prayed a long time for that 'thing,' and God just isn't listening," or "God doesn't speak to me. He speaks to everyone else—but not to me," or, "God doesn't move in my life the way He moves in everyone else's." Let's dive deeper: "God is mean because He took away the person I loved. How could He do that?" Or you've thought, "Why is that person successful and I'm not? God must love them more." All these thoughts are assumptions.

Let's be honest: This is assumption 101. We could go so much deeper than this. Remember what I was assuming at the beginning of this chapter? It was deep. It was embedded in my belief system, and it was all a lie. However, I lived my entire life under the intoxicating influence of that lie. It was a dictator, deciding every move I made. Listen, walking through a season of silence from God is so confusing. It's hard to navigate. But while you meditate on His character and His Word in the silence, this becomes your next step: Don't assume you know what God is doing.

Be your own mind's goalie. Kick out any thought not grounded in truth. Be ruthless. Take every single assumption and every single piece of reasoning about God captive—especially when you're standing in the vacuum of His silence (2 Cor. 10:5).

That morning, in my manager's office, something broke inside me. He became a minister of change in my life. When I left his office to begin my workday, I was still far from God, but I had begun to think about what I was thinking about when it came to Him. My breakthrough was still six months away. But even that morning, I knew I couldn't keep living like that: a paranoid mess.

I knew something had to shift. I had choices to make about my life. I had choices to make about God. Suddenly, I knew that what was going on couldn't continue. I had hit my limit. To this day I believe that God brought me there—to the end of myself.

I believe that old, musty-smelling office is where the

Spirit of the living God began His gentle pursuit of me and where the claws of the enemy's lies began to lose their grip. Assumptions about God had led me there. But God's grace—though hidden at that time—was already moving to bring me out.

Scan this QR code or visit AutumnMilesBooks.com/holyghosted/resources to watch a brief video from me with encouragement and deeper insight for your journey.

Chapter 6
WHAT THE HOLY HEDGE—
DOES GOD PROTECT US?

The LORD *is your protector; The* LORD *is your shade on
your right hand. The sun will not beat down on you by day,
nor the moon by night. The* LORD *will protect you from all
evil; He will keep your soul. The* LORD *will guard your
going out and your coming in from this time and forever.*
—PSALM 121:5–8, NASB

FIELD TRIPS. THE very mention of the word sends a
chill down my spine. Listen, can I have your full permission to speak freely? OK, great. I do *not* like field
trips. I used to—back when I was a new mom and everything felt fresh and new. But over the years, the appeal of
chaperoning a field trip for my beloved children has worn
off. What about the glimmer of herding five to seven children all day under the blazing Texas heat? Yeah, I'm good.
The last time I chaperoned a field trip for Grace was her
fourth-grade visit to the Capitol building in Austin, Texas.

I left with no money and no dignity because I had to
supply lunch for the kids in my group who had forgotten
theirs. Then came the dreaded gift shop. I felt peer-pres-
sured by fourth graders to supply them with "artifacts" as
tokens of remembrance for the ages. The gift shop gets me

every time. I tremble as I approach, knowing the trauma that will surely ensue. Whether it's the smell of "old" when you walk in, the threat of "if you break it, you buy it," or the overpriced trinkets—I can't deal with it. I've had more arguments with my children in gift shops on a field trip than anywhere else.

"Mom, why can't I have the tiny handheld Constitution for $29.99? Don't you like America?"

"Mom, I can't believe you won't buy me a machete knife like the one James Bowie carried when he defended the Alamo. Don't you want me to be a hero like him one day?"

"Mom, I need a $250 replica of the space suit the first female astronaut wore. Don't you want me to be a woman leader just like you?"

For these reasons, and maybe one or two more, I do not like field trips. For the first time, I can admit this, because I finally know that it doesn't make me a bad mom. It makes me a seasoned mom of over twenty years who's learned a thing or two. I adore my four babies desperately—just not their field trips.

Soon enough, another field trip was on the calendar. This time it was a big deal for Moses and Haven—their end-of-year, fourth-grade field trip to Austin, Texas, just as Grace and Jude had before them. The night before the trip, Eddie and I tried everything to convince Moses and Haven to skip the field trip. Because if they didn't go, we didn't have to go. We were only on the hook because we went on Grace and Jude's trip. Moses and Haven, however, quickly played the "That's not fair" card. Haven argued, "You can't not go with us if you went with Grace and Jude! It's not fair." Honestly, my child wasn't wrong. With a sigh and an annoyed glance at Eddie, we packed our bags (so to speak). We were trapped by our integrity. We had to go.

I had one condition: We would not chaperone. We would be responsible only for our own two kids. They agreed happily—sometimes Haven doesn't like people anyway. (Ha!) Eddie and I even resorted to bribery. We offered to let them skip school and to take them to the most prestigious restaurant of all time: their favorite, McDonald's. They didn't budge. So we upped our game. "Listen," we said, "we'll take you to the store and buy your new favorite toy," knowing it would cost less than our mental health (and way less than anything from the dreaded gift shop). Still, nothing. They banded together and stood their ground with every offer. Our efforts failed.

With all that in mind, Eddie and my alarm rang disrespectfully at 4:30 a.m., waking us for yet another field trip. I had already been awake for at least thirty minutes, dreading the day. When the alarm sounded, I flopped my arm over to turn it off and let out the deepest sigh of frustration. I thought, "Here we go again." So at 4:30 a.m., we were headed to Austin. (Yay!)

After packing their pillows, approved handheld devices, and extra lunch, we dropped the kids off at school. Funny enough, the first stop before the Capitol building was a real-life cave. The kids would go on a tour to see what a cave was like. While neat in theory, parents had been informed months in advance that we wouldn't be allowed to enter the cave. We were expected to wait patiently outside while over one hundred kids made their way through the cave. While this didn't sit well with some parents, I was fine with it—because I would rather do just about anything else on earth than be in close proximity to a bat.

Eddie and I finally got into our car, with our piping-hot coffee and equally piping-hot bad attitudes, and off we went. It had rained all night in Dallas, which was one reason why I had been up so early. When a storm hits Texas in the spring, there's a good chance a tornado might tag along. Ever since we moved to Dallas, I've experienced about fifteen tornadoes—seven in one day. So yes, I was a little on edge about the wind and storm as we drove out of the city.

Eddie, half-awake, was driving. I was in the passenger seat, staring out the window and daydreaming about what my day could've been like if Austin hadn't hijacked the schedule. The rain was torrential. Our car shook under the wind, which kept growing stronger. I shifted my body to face the front windshield, grabbed my coffee, and took a sip of the hot nectar from heaven.

We were both silent until my usually laid-back husband slammed on the gas and the car shot forward. From the corner of my eye, I saw a forty- or fifty-foot light pole tipping and beginning to fall. Eddie saw it before I did. We both held our breath as he sped beneath it—going at least eighty miles an hour under a free-falling light pole. Through the sunroof we watched it fall in slow motion. Time seemed to stand still. If we hadn't moved when we did, it likely would've landed on our car and killed us both.

A split second later, I saw the light pole slam to the ground through my back window—just feet behind our car—completely blocking at least three lanes of traffic. The sound was deafening: a violent crash followed by the sharp shatter of glass and then silence. As we drove away, the only thing we could see were headlights—rows of cars that had slammed on their brakes and were now stuck behind the fallen pole.

I didn't turn around right away. I sat frozen, stunned by what had happened—and what might've happened. My mind raced, as I thought, "My four children could now be parentless." When I finally turned to look at Eddie, I just stared. He met my eyes with a shaky voice, "I just saw it falling. I knew it was coming for us. Autumn, that light pole almost killed us." I started shaking. The shock hit me hard. It was too close—way too close.

As we sat in silence, trying to process what just happened, one thing became clear: God had stopped that pole from hitting our car. He had *blocked* it and protected us from a threat we didn't even know existed. If we had left home even one second later, I'm not sure I would be here right now typing this. One second. Do you realize how close that is? One single second could have changed the course of my family's future. Just one.

God stepped in. He allowed Eddie to see what I couldn't: the danger ahead in the darkness. God gave him the wisdom to speed up instead of swerving. If Eddie had turned the wheel, the pole would have hit us. Even though there had been heavy traffic, at that exact moment, no one was around us—nothing to block us from accelerating. The lanes ahead were shockingly clear, just enough for us to maneuver out of the path of destruction.

Yes, God protected us with His hedge of protection and saved our lives that morning as we drove to the field trip.

Yes, You Have a Hedge

You may have heard your grandmama pray it over you, saying something like, "Lord, place a hedge of protection around my grandchild and keep them from the evil one." It's a beautiful, powerful prayer.

What you may not know is that this idea of a "hedge of protection" comes straight from Scripture. The word *hedge* originated in the Book of Job. As previously mentioned, Job is widely accepted by biblical scholars and church historians to be the oldest recorded book in the Bible. So this concept of a divine hedge didn't come from historical tradition; it came from the truth of God's Word.

Now I'm not going to spend time teaching you what you probably already know. But what I *do* want to walk you through is something you may not have noticed before— something revealed neither by Job nor even by God but straight from the mouth of Satan himself. Let me tell you, it's both fascinating and incredibly comforting. If you're a believer in Jesus Christ, you have a hedge of protection surrounding you, and the enemy is completely and fully aware of it.

WHAT EXACTLY DOES A HEDGE DO?

The word *hedge* shows up in modern life in a few different ways. You'll hear it in gardening and in the world of finance. Both are surprisingly relevant when we think about the hedge God places around His people.

In gardening, a hedge is a wall of closely planted bushes or trees. Its main function is to do one thing: create a barrier. That barrier can serve many different purposes such as marking a property line and showing ownership.[1] I see this all the time in Dallas, specifically in Highland Park—a swanky neighborhood right in the heart of the city, where hedges clearly define where one property ends and another begins.

A hedge in gardening is also used for privacy.[2] This is another reason you'll see them in the fancy-dandy neighborhood of Highland Park. The people who live there don't want you looking into their windows or knowing their business.

Yet another purpose is protection. A hedge creates a barrier or a windbreak, shielding what's behind it—like a wall or fence would. It guards what's valuable, and it stands in the way of what doesn't belong.

We also see the word *hedge* used in the world of finance. Now I am no finance expert, but a simple Google search will tell you that a hedge refers to a risk management strategy: an investment used to protect against loss.[3] In other words, it is a strategy to safeguard assets. No one wants to lose money for no reason, and a hedge exists to prevent that. It's a form of financial protection.

Spiritually speaking, Satan's reference to a hedge in the Book of Job beautifully captures both meanings—from gardening to finance. Each one helps us understand the spiritual protection God places around His people. When you consider your life, both these metaphors are worth holding on to.

Let's look at the passage where the word *hedge* first appears. Before diving into the verse itself, let me remind you of the context. In Job 1 Satan comes before God's throne. The Lord asks, "From where do you come?" and Satan answers, "From roaming about on the earth and walking around on it" (Job 1:7). Then God asks, "Have you considered My servant Job?" (Job 1:8).

Now this next part is where things gets fascinating, which is why we will spend more time exploring it. Satan responds, "Does Job fear God for nothing? Have You not made a hedge about him and his house and all that he has, on every side? You have blessed the work of his hands, and his possessions have increased in the land" (Job 1:9–10).

SCRIPTURAL HEDGE

The word *hedge* in Job 1:9 is the Hebrew verb *suk* (pronounced "sook").[4] This specific form appears in only two verses of Scripture, though other tenses of the word appear elsewhere.[5] It means "to hedge up or fence up, to fence about him protectively, to hedge in."[6] In Job's context the hedge wasn't just symbolic; it was a supernatural barrier of God's protection.

Because *suk* is a verb—an action word—we can assume that God actively *built* this hedge around Job. It wasn't something that had always been there. It was created. Constructed. Set into place by God Himself as per Satan's words. God Himself had built a barrier so strong it would be impenetrable by anything or anyone. No person, no enemy, no circumstance could touch Job because the hedge was divinely constructed by God. The only person with the power to penetrate it was God.

Much like the gardening context in which we use the term *hedge*, the scriptural hedge had to be built. When God constructed that hedge around Job, it marked ownership. Everyone—both in the seen and unseen realms—knew Job was one of God's faithful. The hedge created a protective barrier against anything trying to destroy Job.

But I would also argue that the divine hedge of protection around Job created a kind of faith privacy. No one really knew how much faith Job had—not even Job himself—because the hedge kept his faith from being tested. God saw Job's faith, but neither Satan nor Job did. The depth of Job's faith had not yet been revealed because it hadn't been required to endure its harshest test. Until the testing came, even Job didn't know what he carried inside.

Now let's shift to the financial metaphor because the spiritual hedge applies there too. Satan argues with God that He had "made a hedge around him, his house, and all that he has." The hedge didn't just cover Job or his family; it extended to his finances. A divine protection was over Job's resources. No one could deplete what he had because God was managing it. Isn't that interesting?

Satan says, "You have blessed the work of his hands, and his possessions have increased in the land" (Job 1:10). Not only was Job protected from financial loss, but God poured out a supernatural blessing on him. Job's possessions didn't decrease—they increased—because of God's hand of favor and the hedge surrounding him.

Job, his household, his children, and all his assets were protected by the impenetrable hedge God had built. The Creator of the universe—who makes things that last and survive from season to season—also constructed the hedge of protection that Job and his family enjoyed. God knows how to build things that can endure and sustain, and that hedge allowed Job to do so. This is the hedge that we all want. We all long for that same God-built, God-guarded protection surrounding every part of our lives.

THE HEDGE WAS INVISIBLE TO JOB BUT VERY VISIBLE TO SATAN

The question that we all ask—especially after reading Job— is, "Does God really protect me?" The answer is yes. As God's children we have the benefit of His protection. Psalm 121:5–6 (NIV) says, "The LORD watches over you—the LORD is your shade at your right hand; the sun will not harm you by day, nor the moon at night." King David wrote this because he *knew* there was supernatural protection that had guarded him over the years. He could say with confidence that the Lord watches over and protects His people.

David didn't see the hedge over him, but he experienced its effects. He could feel it. Job couldn't see the hedge of protection over him either. Maybe he felt it. Maybe he noticed its effects. But he couldn't physically see it with his plain eyesight.

For example, Eddie and I couldn't see the hedge of protection over us that morning as we drove to Austin, but we saw its effects: The light pole didn't land on us. Eddie felt the quickening in his spirit to move fast. When the pole had fallen, I could feel a rush of peace and gratefulness that God had, in fact, intervened. We can't see the hedge, but we can feel it at times and see its effects.

Because of this passage, which gives us a peek into the throne room of heaven, we know something else: Even if we can't see God's protection, Satan can. He sees the actual hedge and told God, "You have made a hedge of protection around him, his household, and all he has on every side." That truth alone should build our faith.

SATAN HAD CONSIDERED JOB

Let's unpack this. Satan not only saw the hedge but knew how large it was. He knew how vast it was and all that it covered. He had been a student of it. He had studied it. He had measured it. That blows my mind.

When God asked, "Have you considered My servant Job?" the answer was yes—Satan absolutely had. He had looked at every single nook and cranny of the impenetrable hedge and couldn't find a way in. The God-constructed hedge was designed to keep Satan out. Though he searched for a weak spot, his efforts were fruitless. He was completely shut out in the most permanent way. So he gave up. Satan couldn't get in, so it was a lost cause.

How do we know that Satan tried? It's because he knew the hedge's depth, width, and diameter. If there had been any opening—*any way in*—he would've taken advantage of it long before that conversation with God.

That blesses me. As a child of God, I receive that same

divine protection. So do you. It is a benefit of choosing Him as our Father. God builds hedges of protection around us, our children, and everything connected to us—hedges so secure that Satan can't even come close to penetrating them. Even though we can't see these hedges, they are very real. God protects us with something invisible to our eyes but obvious in the spiritual realm. He makes His protection known to the enemy, even if He simply asks us to trust Him. God doesn't need to boast about how awesome His protection is; He just invites us to rest in it. This is why God says confidently more than three hundred times in Scripture, "Do not fear."

With that invitation to trust Him, things like the hedge of protection—things we don't even know we need—are included. There was a moment I was praying through a difficult circumstance and asking God *why* something was happening. He responded to my spirit and said, "Autumn, thank Me for what I didn't allow." That stopped me in my tracks. Thank God for what He didn't allow in your life. Thank Him for the protection He offered without you even knowing there was a threat.

When God said that, I realized: There were things the enemy wanted to stop, plans he tried to sabotage, and weapons he formed against me that God blocked (Isa. 54:17). God gave those attacks no permission to prosper. The enemy tried, but the hedge of protection that God had built around me stopped him.

Take a second, friend, and thank God for what He didn't allow in your life—for the threats you didn't even know were threats and the things that never touched you because God stepped in. He actively protects you every single day, and if we're not careful, we'll forget that. We'll believe the lie that He's distant or uninvolved.

But make no mistake: The enemy knows who has a hedge and who doesn't. If he sees it, he recognizes that barrier as a God-built, impenetrable barrier, and he knows his efforts aren't worth it. He's already lost that battle.

ONE VISIBLE HEDGE TO PICTURE

If you're having trouble believing a hedge of protection surrounds you, there is one passage in Scripture where God's protective hedge is actually *visible*.

Exodus 13:21–22 offers a powerful image. When the people of Israel left Egypt, God went ahead of them in a pillar of cloud by day and a pillar of fire by night. They could see it. When Israel approached the Red Sea, with Pharoah and his entire army closing in behind—the Bible says,

> Then the angel of God, who had been traveling in front of Israel's army, withdrew and went behind them. The pillar of cloud also moved from in front and stood behind them, coming between the armies of Egypt and Israel. Throughout the night the cloud brought darkness to the one side and light to the other side; so neither went near the other all night long.
>
> —EXODUS 14:19–20, NIV

God created a barrier between Israel and the Egyptians. He moved His presence from in front of them to directly between them and their enemy. If the Egyptians wanted to reach Israel, they would have to pass through the pillar of cloud.

God led them with the pillar of cloud and fire, and He protected them too.

Let's read on:

> The Egyptians pursued them, and all Pharaoh's horses and chariots and horsemen followed them into the sea. During the last watch of the night the LORD looked down from the pillar of fire and cloud at the Egyptian army and threw it into confusion. He jammed the wheels of their chariots so that they had difficulty driving. And the Egyptians said, "Let's get away from the Israelites! The LORD is fighting for them against Egypt."
>
> —EXODUS 14:23–25, NIV

This is an incredible visual of what the God-constructed hedge of protection can look like. God sees when the enemy gets close—and He stands in between. God Himself becomes the barrier.

There is a wall you can't see, yet it exists: a spiritual defense system stopping what you may never even know could've been. If you can picture that pillar of cloud and fire, you can imagine God's hedge.

This image should feel like a warm hug.

How often do we worry about our children, finances, or health—and completely omit the fact that God has already placed a hedge over us? We forget that a divine barrier exists between us and evil. Evil can see it, but we often don't.

This is where faith comes in.

The hedge should make you less anxious. The hedge should finally allow you peace. The hedge is real, whether you believe it.

I recently scrolled by a well-known Christian woman with a lot of social media influence. For some reason I stopped and listened. She was interviewing a pastor and asked, "Is there a supernatural world that surrounds us, and we don't even realize it?"

I was dumbfounded. This woman has so much influence, and she's still asking that question. She continued, "Am I actually protected by God, even though I can't see it?"

I wanted to scream through the phone: "Yes, look no further than the Book of Job!"

YES, GOD DOES REMOVE THE HEDGE SOMETIMES

You may ask, "If the hedge protects me, what if God chooses to remove it?" That's a valid, honest question.

There's no denying it: While God does give us divine protection, there are moments when He allows the hedge to be lifted. We see this clearly in Job's life. While that may not be what you want to hear, deep wisdom, insight, and even comfort is hidden in the text about why God may choose to do this—if we're willing to look.

Let's unpack it.

After Satan complained that God's hedge prevented him from attacking Job, he makes a bold assumption about Job: "'But now stretch out your hand and strike everything he has, and he will surely curse you to your face.' The LORD said to Satan, 'Very well, then, everything he has is in your power, but on the man himself do not lay a finger'" (Job 1:11–12, NIV).

Satan believed Job was faithful and upright only because of God's blessings. He claimed that Job was only into his relationship with God for what he got out if it—and that, if it were all taken away, Job would easily give up his faith and curse God. This conversation is deep, because Satan was convinced Job would do what he had seen others do time and time again. He knew human nature. He had used this tactic multiple times before and seen it work. So now *he* was the one assuming, asserting with full confidence that Job's faith was just as shallow and conditional as others. If the blessings stopped, so too would the loyalty.

Is this where you are, sweet friend? I type with a heaviness in my spirit for you. Have you lost something precious? Are you on the verge of giving up on the Lord, whispering, "What's the use? God didn't stop this, so why should I keep serving Him?" I want to take a second and acknowledge your pain. Was it a marriage you lost? Are you left wondering how God could possibly have allowed it? Was it sudden? Or maybe it was a precious child who was taken and now they're with Jesus, and your heart aches in ways you can't even put into words. I am so sorry.

Maybe your loss was financial. Maybe you lost your home, or you're a single mom with no job and no way to make ends meet. Are you waking up at night with anxiety attacks because you can't figure out how to pay the bills? Sister, I grieve with you. These circumstances are absolutely horrific, and I wish I could change them. But friend—*now* through the grief, you have a holy opportunity. You have the chance to silence the one who caused the loss: Satan himself. You get to prove him wrong about you.

As previously mentioned, there are conversations in heaven about us. Right now, the enemy is betting against you. He thinks you'll walk away from God because that's what most people do when faced with something so difficult. He's seen it happen for centuries. But friend, might I console you with this?

I believe that just as Satan measured the length, breadth, and height of the hedge around Job, God was measuring something too—not His hedge but your faith. Satan's betting on you to tap out. He thinks this blow will take you out for good. But God sees what the enemy can't: your faith.

The enemy has no idea how deeply your trust in the Lord runs. But God sees how deep it is. It may feel feeble now, but He sees the deep roots that still exist. He sees how much you've trusted Him over the years. While I have no idea why this has been allowed in your life, I do know this: God has seen that your faith can handle it.

He is the strength to your weakness. Even though your faith feels weak in this moment, He knows that when you completely surrender to His strength, it will be strong enough to get through even this.

God knows His children who can stand the greatest tests and endure to tell of His glory. You, my friend, are the one God chose for this heavy, hard, holy test—not because you're being punished, but because He knows you'll come through it.

He measured your faith before this was allowed. He saw it was sturdy enough to stand—sturdier than Satan assumed and probably sturdier than you feel right now. But this wouldn't have been allowed unless God knew you would still be standing when all else seemed to fail.

HE REMOVES THE HEDGE ONLY A LITTLE AT A TIME

Here's a final encouragement for you, friend: Even in Job's case, the entire hedge of protection wasn't removed all at once. While the enemy was allowed to attack Job—because God knew his faith wouldn't fail—all was not in the enemy's hands. God had already measured what Job's faith could handle, and He set a clear stopping point. God said, "But on the man himself, do not lay a finger." The enemy was given permission but with boundaries.

Satan has a limit; he is on a leash.

God put him on a leash like a dog—he could only go so

far. He can't attack you beyond what your faith can withstand. Why? Because He knows it would be *too much*, and God won't allow *too much*. The enemy does *not* set the limits of the attack. Nope, not him. God does. The devil doesn't have free reign of authority to attack you. His attack has a limit, and it will fail.

He is like a dog on a leash, friend.

Eddie and I made it safely to the underground cave where Moses and Haven were running and playing outside. The first thing Moses said when he saw me was, "Mom, I already ate my entire lunch." Mind you—it was 11 a.m. Then he asked, "Mom, will you get me another lunch?"

My reply was a soft, "Yes, bud, I love you."

As I stood there, alive, I realized I had never been happier to be on a field trip. Going on that field trip—even to the gift shop later that day—I counted as a blessing from God because of His impenetrable hedge over us.

 Scan this QR code or visit AutumnMilesBooks.com/ holyghosted/resources to watch a brief video from me with encouragement and deeper insight for your journey.

Chapter 7
HOLY HONESTY—HOW HONEST
CAN I BE WITH GOD?

*Trust in Him at all times, O people; Pour out your
heart before Him; God is a refuge for us. Selah.*
—Psalm 62:8

A COUPLE OF YEARS ago, I backed out of the driveway
and let out a long sigh of relief. My heart and mind
felt heavy all morning. For months I had strangely
felt that God was against me. I knew that wasn't true. Of
course not—God was for me! I knew that, yet I couldn't
help but feel that way because I had just been passed over for
an opportunity that I had desperately wanted.

I put the convertible into drive and pushed the magic
button that dropped the top. The wind against my face felt
refreshing as I maneuvered the car through the neighborhood, savoring every moment of the sunshine. The Texas
heat on the top of my head felt good. That day I needed an
escape—and that blessed little car was the perfect medicine
for my heavy heart.

I crept through the back streets of our town, knowing
that once I hit the highway into Dallas, all the peace would
evaporate. Sure enough, the traffic didn't disappoint, as I
had to accelerate my speed and deal with the dreaded Dallas

traffic. With every car that zoomed past me, I thought, "No, you cannot have my peace."

After twenty minutes navigating the zoo that is Dallas traffic, my mood began to shift. I found myself in stop-and-go congestion, which was backed up because of an accident still several miles ahead. My mind wandered back to the disappointment I had just faced—another *no*, more rejection. I couldn't understand what was happening. I felt as if God had asked me to take this step of faith only to be rejected. It didn't make any sense to me. Why?

Why would God invite me on this journey only to stop it cold?

I started asking God about it. As I drove down I-30 into Dallas, I prayed, trying to make sense of what God was doing in my life. But I couldn't get a read on what He wanted. I admit, my prayer was weak and way too whiny. Honestly, I felt like one of my kids being passive-aggressive, complaining, "You always do this for him, so why can't you do it for me?" That is a classic line that every mom knows all too well.

I kept asking God to answer my whiny prayer, but He didn't. To fill the silence, I said something like, "It's fine, I guess. I know You love me, and You have a reason." I scrambled for the nauseating, Sunday school, robotic answer—the kind that would've won me a piece of candy in kids' church thirty-plus years ago. "I guess I'm fine with the no," I continued. "I mean, I don't like it, but I trust You."

After blatantly lying to the Lord—telling Him I was fine when I wasn't—I sat in silence, rolling my car through the morning traffic.

Suddenly, I felt a strong impression in my spirit: "That's not how you really feel, is it, Autumn?" I straightened in my seat, adjusted the mirror, and leaned in. God had straight up called me out. I didn't say a word. I just sat there, waiting. Then I felt it again: "That's not how you really feel, is it, Autumn?"

I burst into tears.

"No," I cried. "No, it's not how I really feel." In that moment of raw confession, the Lord followed up with this: "Autumn, tell Me how you really feel."

With full permission from the Lord to release everything, I did just that. I began to speak out the feelings I had tried to stuff down. I felt embarrassed, abandoned, rejected, and so frustrated. No, it wasn't fine. I *wasn't* fine. I was angry.

Do you want to know the truth? I wasn't just angry at the situation; I was mad at God, and He knew it. I had just been too much of a coward to say it. I didn't want God to be angry with me.

Since childhood, I've struggled with the effects of fear theology—this belief that if I'm too honest with God, then He'll punish me for it. If I express frustration or disappointment, then He'll push back or lash out. I didn't want God to be mad at me. I couldn't take that on top of everything else. So I kept quiet. I figured it was safer to pretend. However, because of His fresh invitation to be honest, I finally found the courage to say what I had been hiding.

"God, I'm mad at You. I'm so mad at You."

Then the sobs came.

With the sobs came a great calm in my spirit. There was no harsh rebuke or punishment—just peace.

I surely didn't expect such a great sense of calm and peace.

Still sitting in traffic, I began to empty my heart before the Lord. I poured out every emotion and thought I had suppressed over the past few months. The Lord's invitation to speak freely was exactly what my entire being needed. I needed an emotional reset, and the Lord Himself had created a safe space for me to release my suppressed thoughts, allowing me to move forward. It was a great cleansing—a sacred unraveling. Through it I realized this: God had positioned me to be completely honest with Him. That was what He wanted all along: intimacy with me.

Job Had the Strength to Be Honest

The Book of Job has inspired me—and, if I'm honest, puzzled me—for years, mostly because of the brutal honesty Job had with the Lord. Part of me is in awe. I've always wanted that kind of freedom in my relationship with God. Another part of me cringes and wonders, "Am I allowed to be that honest with Him?"

Job was real. He didn't sugarcoat his pain or try to protect God's feelings; he just said it like it was. In some ways he called God out:

> I cry out to You for help, but You do not answer me;
> I stand up, and You turn Your attention against me.
> You have become cruel to me; with the might of
> Your hand You persecute me. You lift me up to the
> wind and cause me to ride; and You dissolve me in
> a storm. For I know that You will bring me to death
> and to the house of meeting for all living.
> —Job 30:20–23

Do you see what I mean?

As we all clutch our religious pearls, let's remember—Job's grief was great. His exhaustion overtook him. His suffering is something most of us—save for Jesus—will never be asked to endure all at once. It was debilitating, and it wore down the veneer of his faith.

The shiny, small-group answers were gone. Suffering had chiseled away the plaster of counterfeit pleasantries and forced the raw, unfiltered truth to pour out of him like sewage. Sometimes the truth is ugly. Truth—though ugly, unpleasing, and even grotesque—is still truth.

GOD DESIRES TRUTH, EVEN IF IT IS UGLY

God desires truth. He desires truth from us. He doesn't want to be talked to like He's your Sunday school teacher; He wants the unvarnished version of where you are emotionally, mentally, and spiritually. Anything less is dishonesty.

He is the way, the truth, and the life. As previously mentioned, He is the *truest of truth*. He deals in the truth, and when we offer Him our honest thoughts and feelings, He can lead us forward.

God reminds me of this when I'm tempted to lie to Him about how I feel. This verse pries honesty right out of me: "Behold, You desire truth in the innermost being, and in the hidden part You will make me know wisdom" (Ps. 51:6).

The Word of God constantly reminds us to speak truth. Ephesians 4:15 tells us to ensure we are "speaking the truth in love." Ephesians 6:14 (NIV) reminds us to put on the "belt of truth." Speaking the truth is so important to the Lord, it even made the top ten. One of the Ten Commandments says, "You shall not bear false witness against your neighbor" (Exod. 20:16). Or in plainer terms, it means: Don't lie. Psalm 34:13 chimes in too: "Keep your tongue from evil and your lips from speaking deceit."

I could go on and on with verses that charge us to speak truth, but I'm sure you get the point.

So let me ask you this: If God desires truth in the inward parts of us, so much so that He repeats it throughout

Scripture, wouldn't He want us to be truthful with Him—even when it's an ugly truth?

True intimacy with the Lord comes when we operate in truth with Him.

A few years ago, I was asked to take on the role of Volunteer Pastor of Women's Prisons in the state of Texas for my church. I was to oversee planting churches in women's prisons across Texas. I was so honored. To this day it may be one of my favorite assignments God has asked me to say yes to.

My oversight pastor had arranged a meet and greet at the first prison where I would be working. Meetings with both the inmates and the staff were scheduled separately. My goal that day was to get a feel for the spiritual needs of these women in prison. From a girl who has never been to prison, listening was at the top of my agenda for our meeting.

The warden and chaplain of the prison had selected a group of thirty incarcerated women to meet with me and my oversight pastor. Eddie came with me as well.

The process of entering a prison for the first time was quite an education. I had to surrender all my belongings—my ID, everything. I was searched and scanned and was on high alert as I prepared to meet the ladies. My mood was somber as I stepped into the designated meeting room inside the prison walls.

You don't just walk into a room in prison; you wait for permission to do every single task—things we barely give thought to outside those walls. The three of us walked in. Eddie and I were definitely a little more timid than the pastor who accompanied us. One by one, the women began to enter the meeting area. I stood to greet each of them with a smile and a gentle, "Nice to meet you."

Each of the female inmates were kind to me. Maybe they could feel my anxiety—or read the imaginary sign above my head that said, "I'm scared; I've never done this before." Their grace put me at ease within minutes.

I began the meeting with a peppy, "I've never been to prison, but I'm so happy to be here." The ladies gave me a mercy laugh, as if to say, "We got you." With pen and paper in hand, I told them our goal was to plant a church inside the prison. I explained that my understanding was they would be the ones to lead it. Then I asked, "What are the emotional and spiritual needs of the women at this prison?" My goal was to try to meet them, so I added, "Please be honest with us. We can't meet your needs if you aren't."

I didn't know what to expect. Maybe I was naive. I was green in my experience with prison ministry. I expected veneer, polish—masked responses like the ones I've been programmed to hear in the world of women's ministry. I brace for them. I've even become an expert at challenging them, pushing past programmed responses to collect true, honest thoughts. It's a thrill of mine.

I sat perched in my chair like a catcher at a Little League game—glove out, ready for my first pitch. I thought I was prepared for whatever might be thrown my way, but I certainly wasn't expecting a curveball of *truth*. I didn't expect the rawness—the lack of varnish. I braced for the fake and the phoniness and for the programmed answers heard for years in ministry circles. But this was different. This was new. This was a full-on truth bomb.

For three hours I stayed perched—listening—as one comment after another came, each one indicting the state of the Western church and the way these women have come to view God.

They made statements such as, "No church that comes

stays—they get tired of us," "We trust no one, and we won't trust you for a while," and "I hate fake Christians. If you come, we'll smell the fake on you." One woman asked, "Will you leave like everyone else? We've been abandoned our whole lives." But another question stopped me cold. I leaned in and asked multiple follow-up questions. "Will you betray us too?"

I've learned over the years to be slow to speak and quick to listen (Jas. 1:19). This wasn't a room that needed to know how much theology I knew or biblical knowledge I had—it was a room that needed to know how much I cared about people. These women weren't going to hear a single word I said until they felt like I truly saw them and until they knew I actually cared.

There could be no moving forward in ministry with these precious inmates until a foundation of truth and transparency was established. It hit me—almost to the point of tears—that maybe no one had ever let them be *this* brutally honest before—not about the Lord, not about their experiences with the church, and not about their relationship with God.

As I went down the list of about thirty women, it became clear that they all desperately wanted the same thing: truth, transparency, and authenticity—from me and, ultimately, in their walk with God. If what we offered didn't include those three things, they had no interest.

They, like Job, were too grieved for the pleasantries and had been through too much for the fake.

At the end of the meeting, I sat back in my chair, surrounded by those women, and I thanked them. I wasn't offended by their honesty—not in any sense of the word. I was inspired by it. Their honesty gave me the context I needed to understand the spiritual needs of those ladies more effectively, and consequently the entire prison.

Their honesty, though sometimes ugly and raw, gave birth to something beautiful.

I sat and listened. I heard what they had been waiting to say to someone for maybe years. When I thanked them on the way out, they began to thank me, Eddie, and my oversight pastor for the opportunity to speak and be a voice for the inmates.

When God tells us that He desires truth, I thought, "*This must be why.*"

The raw truth from those ladies was freeing for them and life-changingly helpful for me. It gave me context for my relationship with the Lord. He desires truth even if it's ugly—especially then—because truth from us builds intimacy with Him. Truth creates the kind of connection that wouldn't be possible without it.

I realized something else too: When the truth is hard, it hurts me more to say it than it hurts God to hear it. He is not offended by my honesty; He delights in it. Over and over, in Scripture, He asks for our truth. So why don't I give it—even in my most vulnerable prayers? Because it's not Him the truth hurts; it's me. It's my pride—my pride in how strong I think my faith should be or how strong I wish it were.

THE ENEMY ATTACKS HONESTY IN OUR RELATIONSHIP WITH GOD

Even small dishonesty with the Lord is still dishonesty, and it keeps us from experiencing true transparency with God. Satan will try to convince us that being halfway truthful is good enough. But in our relationship with the Lord, perhaps no attack is greater than the one aimed at our transparency.

If the enemy can get us to second-guess being fully honest with God, he can keep us from the true intimacy with God our hearts were made for. The question "Can I really be that honest with God?" was born in hell itself. Hell wants a barrier between you and the Lord—a barrier built quietly and subtly through the absence of truth in the "inward parts" with your Creator.

Satan, the father of lies (John 8:44), wants to influence your relationship with the One who is faithful and true (Rev. 19:11). The enemy doesn't just accuse you before God; he accuses God to you. He plants doubts that make you hold back in your relationship with the Lord.

For example, he may attack your honesty with God by tempting you to believe that God will be angry if you're truly transparent—much like he did with me, making me believe God is some mean and wrathful being. Or he might whisper that certain things are too disrespectful to bring up with God—that He wouldn't like it if you talked to Him that way. He may even tempt you to believe that being fully honest about what you're facing somehow means you lack faith in God's plan or His goodness.

We are tempted.

When we give in to those thoughts, we dilute the raw, unedited version of how we feel or think—and unknowingly block the fullness of intimacy with the Lord.

Everything in your life should be brought before the Lord in truth.

There should be a freedom to bring it all—and I mean every single thing—before Him. Bring it all: lust, jealousy, anger, thoughts of divorce, trauma faced in detail, confusion about what He is doing, hatred in your heart, or anything you deem as "inappropriate." All these things can be brought before the Lord. They should be.

When you develop that kind of freedom in your relationship with Him—where nothing is off limits and everything is processed with God—wisdom begins to take root. The truest kind of intimacy grows with the only One who can counsel you through it all—perfectly. Satan hates this intimacy because it erases barriers between you and the Lord instead of building them. He wants obstacles between you and God; God wants them erased by truth.

It's interesting to me that Job is widely accepted as the oldest book in the Bible—and Job's raw honesty with God is on full display. It's as if God was making a point at the very beginning: He wanted us to know that He desires raw truth from us. We can be completely honest with Him, and this version of honesty will not be rejected—because ultimately Job wasn't rejected.

David exemplifies this as well. First and Second Samuel recount many of his victories and his hard-fought conquests. But what about the Psalms? The Psalms are full of his raw thoughts on full display. They're full of his "truth in the inward parts," as he so eloquently puts it (Ps. 51:6, NKJV).

First and Second Samuel are why we love King David so much, but the inward dialogue with God in the Psalms is why we identify with him. He says what we sometimes hesitate to say; he speaks the ugly truth that gives our emotions words. The pages of raw honesty and pure intimacy in the Psalms are the very reason David's conquests were victorious.

THE CHURCH HAS TAUGHT A SORT OF SUPPRESSION THEOLOGY

Growing up in church, I was taught that we couldn't voice certain things to the Lord or we would risk His wrath. True frankness with the Lord was frowned on, and there was an underlying message that you couldn't be honest. You had to walk on verbal eggshells to please Him.

There was no actual Scripture to support this. In fact, quite the contrary—God *desires* truth from us. But it was implied: You could make God mad just by asking questions about things that confused you or by questioning His workings in your life. Questions equaled disrespect.

I know that my church growing up wasn't the only one that promoted this type of suppressive theology. In other words, you might need to suppress your thoughts to remain in good standing with God. Asking questions didn't just equal disrespect; it indicated you lacked true faith.

I would often wonder things about God and the Bible or have strong feelings about Him, but I would stop myself from asking the Lord—just to "stay in His good graces." In reality, this was how Satan kept me from true intimacy with the Lord during that time in my life.

The spirit of dishonesty has infiltrated the church through the idea that you dare not be *too* honest with God or the results could be catastrophic. I watched church leaders judge members who were too transparent about their thoughts or the challenges they faced. I experienced being shunned from the church because of my own transparency.

I learned by watching church leaders, and somewhere in my psyche I decided: "If church leaders didn't accept people being honest with God, then God must not accept them either."

If this was your experience too, this chapter is for you.

I believe a large part of why people leave the church today—whether through deconstruction or for any other reason—is because they don't believe they can have both doubt *and* faith. They think they can't struggle in certain areas with God like Job did and still be counted as righteous. They don't understand that you can ask hard questions and still be accepted by Him.

What we need to teach from our pulpits and small groups is quite the opposite: Bring it all to the Lord and sort it out with Him.

God is our ultimate safe place.

GOD NEVER REBUKES JOB FOR HIS HONESTY

Throughout the Book of Job, it is clear that Job spoke freely. He didn't sanitize his words or operate in fear of making God mad by being honest. He hadn't been taught to suppress his thoughts before the Lord. He had the freedom to talk openly and transparently. He told the truth of how he felt to the Lord—even when the truth was ugly.

Scripture says something beautiful about this: "Through all this Job did not sin nor did he blame God" (Job 1:22). This stopped me.

After reading all of Job's responses, I was surprised by this verse. But then I read this one too: "In all this Job did not sin with his lips" (Job 2:10, NKJV).

I've considered the broader context of Job. I've read the book several times and studied it at length, and the text tells us plainly, "Job did not sin with his lips." This tells us something about our gracious God: He wants to hear the truth from us.

You've heard the saying, "You can't handle the truth," but God can.

Speaking the truth will never be sinful.

It's also interesting that God never rebukes Job for his honesty or questions—not once in the entire book. Not. One.

Time. You won't find it. He never says anything to stop Job from speaking transparently to Him. He welcomed it. It may sound harsh, but as we see in Job, it was rooted in truth.

Dear friend, you are human—and God knows that. You are allowed to be angry. You are allowed to express your emotions. I want you to take a moment and begin the process of purifying your conversations with God, focusing only on truth.

This may sound silly but go with your girl on this one: When you pray, pour out everything—raw and real—to the Lord. Be careful of the temptation to sanitize your prayers. Please don't edit your prayers based on what you *think* He wants to hear. Let your truth flow like a river from your heart.

The most effective conversations that I've ever had with the Lord were the ones when I didn't hold back—when I poured out everything like a drink offering before Him. It has been during my ugliest moments that He begins to mend and heal the hard places in my heart.

He has never rejected me. He has never told me to stop. He has only drawn me in—just as I do with my children when they need to process something—and He has comforted me.

Chances are, you grew up in a church like I did—one more focused on rules than matters of the heart. Like me, you may have been taught that true honesty with God is dangerous.

Friend, that's a lie.

There is no safer place than Jesus. He can handle our transparency and even our ugly truth. He isn't intimidated by honesty; He wants you to process everything *with* Him, not apart *from* Him.

Even as I type, I can hear Him calling out to you:

"Are you weary of carrying it all?"

"Are you tired of not having a safe place to process difficult situations?"

He is that safe place, friend. Come home to Him. Tear down the barrier.

Scan this QR code or visit AutumnMilesBooks.com/ holyghosted/resources to watch a brief video from me with encouragement and deeper insight for your journey.

Chapter 8
THE HOLY ANSWER IS BEING UNANSWERED—WHEN THE ANSWER IS NO ANSWER

Jesus answered and said to him, "What I do you do not realize now, but you will understand hereafter."
—JOHN 13:7

I BIT MY CHEEK hard to avoid tears streaming down my face. It was an early September morning, and our home was filled with the chaos of four children getting ready for school. School mornings are like the ultimate tornado, hurricane, tsunami, earthquake, and every other natural disaster. They're fast, furious, full of a sense of urgency and sometimes terror—and then, just as quickly, they're over, and calm resumes.

With four children in school at the time—one senior, one sophomore, and two in second grade—I was exhausted by 7:30 a.m. every single morning.

Jude, my oldest son, has kept my prayer life alive and active throughout his life. He's always at the top of my prayer list. Jude is the child who has struggled with his health for as long as I can remember. From the age of one, he suffered from what was diagnosed as asthma and severe allergies, resulting in a horrific barking cough that continued well into his teen years.

At this point he was taking four daily medications and dared not go anywhere without a rescue inhaler close by. With Jude we've encountered multiple severe emergencies—episodes that escalated so quickly we've almost lost him several times. His asthma attacks can be sudden, and in his case cause his throat to close within minutes.

After fifteen years of managing his symptoms, Eddie and I have become experts on our son's health—sometimes more so than his doctors. I've often called the doctor's office to correct a dosage or recommend a medication change during an episode. Knowing his medical history, even his doctors acknowledge that we—his parents—often have more insight.

During the summer of Jude's sophomore year, his health took a turn for the worse. He wasn't just battling severe asthma and allergy symptoms anymore; his whole body seemed to be giving out. His immune system weakened, and he weakened with it. During that summer, he was diagnosed with a foot infection that, even after three months of treatment, he couldn't kick. Despite multiple medications, his body just wouldn't heal.

He was making regular trips to the doctor for colds and other ailments, needing extra medications just to stay functional. By the time the first day of school arrived, I felt a heavy urgency to pray for his body. I sensed the enemy using the attack on Jude's physical health as a deeper attack on his mind, which was exactly what Satan was after: his faith.

Weeks into Jude's sophomore year, right smack dab in the middle of a harsh football season, he came home one day and said, "Mom, these spots on my arm are itchy—like bug bites. Do you know what they are?" Taking a quick glance, I dismissed them as bug bites and went about my day. A week later, the "bug bites" had grown larger. They looked more concerning, and they were multiplying. It seemed like a new lesion appeared almost daily.

Jude has always been a trooper when it comes to his health. Unfortunately, he's had to learn how to live with feeling sick much of the time. But that week something shifted—he told me his body felt more tired than usual. He even said it felt like his own body was fighting against itself.

I took him back to the doctor, who referred us to another specialist, who then sent us to a third doctor to run tests on the lesions. Meanwhile, they kept growing. They were uncomfortable—itching, burning, bright red—and Jude was completely miserable. After several days of waiting, we finally received a diagnosis: staph infection. But it wasn't just any staph infection—within days we found out it was the worst kind he could have. We started aggressive treatment and medication immediately.

I resumed my role as Jude's mom-nurse—a role I knew well after fifteen years of his chronic illnesses. The diagnosis was new, but the role was the same: nurse. He needed me to reassure him that everything would be OK with his health, even when, at times, I quietly wondered.

One of the doctor's instructions was to keep Jude's wounds clean and bandaged with fresh dressings twice a day. That morning marked about six weeks of doing just that: dressing his wounds every single day. My optimism had worn thin. My desperation for the Lord to intervene was at an all-time high.

Slowly, I peeled off the old bandages to assess the state of the wounds. They were healing slowly, but it felt like whenever one lesion improved, another would appear. It was maddening. The wear and tear on Jude's body was beginning to affect both our minds.

As I applied the antibiotic ointment, Jude quietly asked,

"Mom, why isn't God taking this away?" I said nothing. He began to break down. "Mom, I have asked God to heal me so many times, and it just seems like my body is getting worse and worse." I kept dressing his wounds. "Mom, why isn't God acting? I need Him to heal me. I don't want to do this anymore."

Tears streamed down his face. He broke.

Even for my six-foot-tall son, it was too much. The attack on his body had finally broken through his mental strength. He rarely complains, so I knew in that moment—deep in my spirit—he didn't need comfort from me. He needed comfort from God Himself.

I've learned in motherhood that sometimes silence is the best response. Overreacting could cause damage; underreacting could do the same. Silence indicates nothing and supports nothing. So I stood silent for a moment, not wanting to agree or disagree with Jude, even though his words had been the cry of my own heart for the past month.

It's horrific to watch your child suffer for years—to the point of death more than once—and be powerless to intervene. I had prayed. I had faith. I had read Scripture over his body. I had prophesied to his flesh, surrendered, and cried out to God. I had everyone I know pray over him. I did everything I knew how to do spiritually. I had faith—I truly had it.

I had also exhausted every single medical option suggested to us. If someone recommended one, down the rabbit trail we would go—until it, too, became another dead end. I had done it all, and I was at the end. To date, there has been *nothing* harder for me to walk through than watching my child suffer for a decade and a half. Nothing.

When you watch your child suffer, all you want is to hear from God. No one else's words will do. Nothing soothes the place inside you that is desperate for comfort. A chorus of bystanders offered their "Let go and let God." These were trite, shallow encouragements that fell on deaf ears. I had tuned them out years ago. The "Just have more faith" ensemble most likely has never had a chronically ill child. They most likely haven't stayed up night after night trying anything and everything to soothe their child's suffering—because I couldn't take it away.

Some days I wanted them to take their encouragement and shove it. It was empty, inauthentic, and lacked even an ounce of empathy.

I identified with the Shunammite woman as she sprinted to Elisha after her son collapsed from head trauma. I understood Jairus in Scripture when he sought out Jesus and begged Him to go to his house and heal his daughter. We needed a touch from God. Jude needed a touch. Just one touch, and I knew he would be healed.

But even though I tarried long in prayer, the healing hadn't come.

My questions mirrored Jude's, and to this day, God had been silent.

I blinked multiple times, trying to blink away the tears that wanted to be set free from the bondage of my eyelids. They had been waiting to come. They *needed* to come, but I stopped them so my son could preserve even a sliver of peace that we both desperately needed.

As I bandaged his arm that morning, I had nothing to say. For all my studying and theological training, no theological book or brilliant mind can truly explain why the innocent suffer. People much older and wiser than me—those with impressive degrees and spiritual depth—still can't explain it. Of course, they speculate—but speculation is just that: speculation, not fact. If anyone truly knew why

God permits it, the answer would be preached from every pulpit every single weekend.

It's the head-scratcher that we all want clarity on.

A myriad of theories exist—and then again, none at all. It's higher than us. Our reasoning can't process it.

I wish I had the answer that day, but I didn't. I had no comfort to offer. I knew a great deal about God's character, His Word, and His presence, but I didn't have an answer for *this*: the relentless suffering.

After minutes of silence, as my teenage son's damp eyes looked at me for an answer, I simply said, "Son, I don't know." The air was heavy. My voice was steady but honest: "I don't know." I wouldn't play pretend for him. He knew I didn't know either.

Collecting myself as I finished bandaging his arm, I added, "I don't know why you are suffering, but God does. What I *do* know about God is that I can trust Him with His reasoning."

My teary-eyed, suffering son looked at me and simply said, "OK, Mom," then took a deep, cleansing breath—as if surrendering fully to whatever God was doing in his life.

The "I don't know" answer had to be enough, because that was all I had.

THE ANSWER IS NO ANSWER

Please bear with me as I attempt to tackle the subject of why innocent people suffer. I'm aware that some of you may be reading this book for this chapter alone. Perhaps your faith is hanging in the balance because you think you *need* an answer for why God has allowed something hard in your life—and it hasn't come.

We all want answers.

We all want to know why God allows suffering.

We all want clarity.

But I think part of the answer isn't found in what we *don't* know about God but in what we *do know about Him*. What we know for certain about God tells us a lot about the mystery of what we *don't* know. When you have to answer your son, as I did, with a hard "I don't know," you can always follow up with what you *do* know. Before we explore that, let's settle something: Sometimes the answer truly is that there is no answer. God may not answer the questions that are plaguing you.

I find it fascinating that, in the oldest book in the Bible—Job—God sets a precedent even before the rest of Scripture is written. The first precedent? That the righteous do suffer. The second? That sometimes God doesn't give a reason.

God told us, centuries before Jesus arrived, that the righteous are allowed to suffer—as if to pave the way for His Son. He let us know up front that He allows suffering, and He will allow it again through Jesus' sacrifice.

Because of the Book of Job, we know this truth about God: He allows suffering. Jesus and Job are powerful examples of this.

Regarding the second precedent God sets in Job: He doesn't always reveal *why* He allows certain things. Remember, God was silent for the first thirty-seven chapters of Job. When He finally speaks in Job 38, He still doesn't answer Job's questions.

In the previous chapter, I discussed at length that you can be raw and honest with God without expecting Him to answer every question. In fact, He has a history of *not* answering our questions.

Let's get into it.

In Judges 6 God visits Gideon. The people of Israel were

getting ransacked by their enemies—the Midianites—to the point of terror. They were hiding in mountain clefts, caves, and strongholds, scattered in every direction, and in many ways humiliated and afraid. When they cried out to the Lord for help, He chose Gideon as their leader.

When God appears to Gideon while he was threshing wheat in the winepress, He says, "The LORD is with you, O valiant warrior" (Judg. 6:12).

When Gideon he heard this, he began to question the Lord. In verse 13 (NKJV), he says,

> Oh my lord, if the LORD is with us, why then has all this happened to us? And where are all His miracles which our fathers told us about, saying, "Did not the LORD bring us up from Egypt?" But now the LORD has forsaken us and delivered us into the hands of Midianites.

We all can relate to Gideon's questions: "Why is this happening?" and "Where are those miracles that we've heard so much about?" But God doesn't answer him. Scripture says that the Lord looked at him, heard every one of his questions, and rather than responding with answers, He responded with encouragement: "The LORD looked at him and said, 'Go in this your strength and deliver Israel from the hand of Midian. Have I not sent you?'" (Judg. 6:14). It seems as if God completely ignored his questions and gave no answer.

Like Job, God didn't answer any of Gideon's questions. In His wisdom He left them unanswered. This isn't unusual in Scripture; God often looks past the questions people ask. For example, Moses had many questions about his call to lead Israel out of bondage, but God didn't directly address most of them. Jesus, in the New Testament, did the same in

His interactions with the crowds, Pharisees, and Sadducees, seemingly ignoring many questions. But did God truly ignore them? While it is true that specific questions were left unanswered, God never ignores them. God may not answer in the way we expect, but He always responds. His responses to our questions are often more beneficial than direct answers. Let me explain.

To Gideon, God responded with a charge of encouragement. To Moses, He responded with displays of power and reaffirmed that Moses was chosen. In the New Testament, Jesus often responded with parables or stories to illustrate His point. While God may not always answer the question, He has a long history of responding.

WHY DOES GOD LEAVE QUESTIONS UNANSWERED?

This may not be something you want to hear, but let's dive in—you may feel differently. Why doesn't God answer all our questions directly? Why would He respond without giving us the answer we're asking for? Because He knows that's not actually what you need from Him. God often refrains from answering because He's not focused on the audible question; He's listening to the deeper longing beneath it. He looks past our words and sees our soul. His eyes see what we need to know. He isn't limited by what we want to hear.

Most of the time, our questions are just symptoms of deeper spiritual needs. We think we need an explanation, but what our hearts truly need is comfort. Let me ask: If God handed you a full report, bullet-pointed to perfection, explaining exactly why He allowed this particular situation in your life, would it change anything in you? Would it bring you peace?

Would it heal your pain? The thing still happened. The loss still came. Is that truly what you're looking for?

If God hasn't answered your question, perhaps that's because an answer isn't what you truly need. Perhaps the question is just a signal pointing to something deeper. We ask questions when what we're really craving is unconditional love. We ask questions when what we need is peace. We ask questions when what we really long for is assurance—that God sees us and that He's still with us.

God knows an answer may not be what your soul is actually longing for. That's why He responds to the deeper spiritual need, not just the surface-level inquiry. He knows what you truly need, even if you don't. God always responds—but He doesn't always answer. More often than not, what you're seeking isn't truly an answer at all—it's the comfort, peace, love, and reassurance that He's still with you.

WHY DOES GOD RESPOND BUT NOT ANSWER?

While I'm sure there are many reasons God responds to our spiritual needs rather than answering our specific questions, I want to focus on just one: To be plain and simple, it's because some of His reasons wouldn't make sense to us.

If you're a parent, you've experienced this. Your young child asks you a question that they *want* answered, but they're too young to process it. For example, as a mom of four, each of my kids is different, yet every single one of them asked me around five years old, "Mom, where do babies come from?" They were curious, wanted answers, and fully expected me to deliver. But at that age, they simply weren't ready for a full, detailed answer. They wouldn't have understood it. It would've been too much for them to process.

So instead of going into the biological details of how babies are made and where they come from, I said something like, "I'll tell you when you're a little older and ready to understand." You've most likely done the same. Why do we do this? Because the truth would've been more than they could handle at that age. They wouldn't have understood it.

In the Book of Job, God never tells Job why he suffers. He never answers the questions Job asks—but rest assured, there was a reason (or reasons) God allowed it. Just as my kids wouldn't understand the answer to where babies come from at the age of four or five, Job wouldn't have understood God's reasoning for the harsh trials he endured either. There was a good reason. We aren't allowed to suffer for sport. God is good. He would never allow relentless suffering without purpose. But if He gave us His reasoning, it's almost certain we wouldn't understand. Why? Because God doesn't make decisions based on human logic. He makes his decisions based on supernatural wisdom that far exceeds anything we could comprehend.

Human questions want human answers. God allows suffering in situations where no reason is given—even though one exists—because we wouldn't be able to process His divine reasoning. Scripture puts it this way: "For who has known the mind of the LORD, that he will instruct Him?" (1 Cor. 2:16). We don't know the mind of God. We aren't His equal, and we don't instruct Him—because we wouldn't even understand how. He operates on a divine level; we operate on a human one.

Isaiah says something similar: "'For My thoughts are not your thoughts, nor are your ways My ways,' declares the LORD. 'For as the heavens are higher than the earth, so are My ways higher than your ways and My thoughts than your thoughts'" (Isa. 55:8–9). We often quote this verse, but really grasping its meaning gives us perspective on why He leaves questions unanswered. His ways and thoughts are higher—far beyond what we can process or comprehend.

Romans chimes in too: "Oh, the depth of the riches and wisdom and knowledge of God! How unsearchable are his judgements and how inscrutable his ways!" (Rom. 11:33, ESV). In 1 Corinthians 2:9, Scripture says that what God has planned for us has never even entered the human heart—no eye has seen it, nor has an ear heard it. Friend, His reasons are real, but they are far beyond our understanding.

A solemn peace comes over me when I think about the fact that a divine reason exists for why my son has suffered for fifteen years—a reason only God understands. After walking intimately with the Lord for twenty-three years, that's good enough for me. If God has reasons—even though it has been horrific—I trust Him. If He knows, I don't have to know. Since God allowed it and knows why, I don't have to know why. I surrender my desire to know why to the supernatural wisdom of God.

WAYS THAT GOD RESPONDS

We've established that God may not answer your questions—because His mind isn't like ours. His supernatural logic is often beyond what we can understand. However, what He always does is respond.

He responded to Job. He responded to Gideon. He responded to Moses. He responds to you—with what He sees you truly need.

God responds in many ways. His response may come as comfort. It may come as clarity of purpose. It may be a new perspective you hadn't thought of. He might respond with an open door or a new opportunity. Sometimes He responds with a period of waiting. Sometimes He may also respond with a process.

There are countless ways our souls cry out and just as many ways God chooses to respond. One way He often responds is with a promise.

After God responded to Gideon with comfort, He followed with a promise: "Surely I will be with you, and you shall defeat Midian as one man" (Judg. 6:16). Gideon needed reassurance. He was scared and overwhelmed. He needed to know he wouldn't face the impossible alone. That promise was exactly what his heart needed.

We ask God questions for all kinds of reasons. Just as He knows why He allows hardship, He also knows *why* we ask what we ask. He sees through the questioning, meets the *root* of the cry with His wisdom, and responds with exactly what our souls need.

DON'T LET THE LACK OF AN ANSWER KEEP YOU FROM GOD

Years ago my husband and I met a wealthy businessman. He was married to his second or third wife and had many children, resulting in a blended family. He spoke to us at length about their family activities on Sundays. Sunday was a huge family day for them, and he seemed to genuinely cherish the time they spent together.

When he found out that Eddie was a pastor, he immediately started backtracking about their Sundays. It was as if he felt the need to justify why they didn't attend church. (Side note: Don't feel like you have to confess your lack of church attendance to a pastor.) Pastors, at least gracious ones, aren't judging you for not showing up. Yes, they always want you there but not out of obligation. They know the spiritual health that comes from being in God's presence and surrounded by His people. We get it; we're human too. (PS: I've skipped some Sundays as well.)

OK, let's go back to the story.

I remembered this particular man for one reason: He used to be a pastor but eventually left the church and even left his relationship with God. The complex trials he faced in life became too much to reconcile. The bottom line was that he couldn't make sense of them. He asked God many questions, but he never felt like he received any answers. His need for understanding overtook him; as a result, he gave up on both the church at large and his relationship with God.

Stories like this grieve me because I know there are thousands—possibly millions—more just like it. When tragedy strikes a family or an individual, there often seems to be a profound silence from God. Questions go unanswered, and in that silence, bitterness and anger take root. I get it. I've been tempted to leave the faith too. I've wanted to throw in the towel on God.

But if I were to simply walk away because I didn't receive an answer from God about a particular situation in my life, I'd be giving up the most incredible gift I've ever received: His grace in salvation. I'd be forfeiting the future I know He's planned for me and surrender the single most incredible relationship of hope I've ever known. The miracles would cease. The joy would cease. Shall I go on?

What about me? An answer just isn't worth that.

I'm getting emotional as I type because I know some of you are right at the edge. You're at the point of giving up on God because the pain is too great.

You blame God. Your soul is crying out for answers, but none are coming. Instead, you need to seek a *response* from God—not an answer. Watch for it. Open His Word and ask the Holy Spirit to lead you to the very thing your soul is longing for. Scripture says, "You will seek Me and find Me when you search for Me with all of your heart" (Jer. 29:13). The next verse declares, "'I will be found by you,' declares the LORD" (Jer. 29:14).

You will find Him. You will find His response.

He will respond because His Word assures us that He is with us and He sees us. So call out to Him. Cry out to Him. God doesn't promise an answer, but He will respond with His presence.

When my son's arm was completely healed, I went on a medical expedition for his health. Those few months with Jude became the catalyst for an aggressive retaliation against his illness. While we had done everything we were told to do, I was convinced there was more that we needed to know. Jude and I began a long journey to find out why all this was happening to him.

In the months that followed, I took Jude to numerous doctors, and they ran countless tests. Meanwhile, in the middle of this medical rollercoaster, Jude was on a spiritual expedition of his own. Rather than giving up on God—because he felt shortchanged by life—he began pressing into the Lord, seeking His response. We were both pressing forward aggressively: I, on the medical front, and Jude, on the spiritual one.

I wish I could explain to you how what happened next came to be, but once again—I have no answer.

We were matched with an immunologist, one of the best in Dallas–Fort Worth. Like all the others, he began running tests, but each batch started to come back completely normal—except for one. Jude's lungs were functioning at 100 percent. For the first time in his life, he had no known allergies. We even repeated multiple blood tests to confirm. He had no signs of cancer. His immune system came back to normal. With every visit we got better news than the last.

The only thing detected was a congenital defect in his immune system: a condition present since birth. That was it. Absolutely nothing else.

At the same time, Jude's health began to improve dramatically. After he completed treatment for the infection, he stopped getting sick every month. His body grew stronger, and suddenly the medical tests showed what we had never seen before: a healthy boy.

But here's the remarkable thing: He had never been healthy. The tests didn't align with his medical history—not even close.

During this time, on Jude's spiritual journey, he attended a winter camp with our church. After praying and diligently seeking the Lord, he finally received a response from Him. It wasn't an answer, but it was a response. The word God gave Jude was *fire*.

As he retells the story, that was the moment when God gave him clarity about his future, and for the first time a sense of purpose emerged from his pain. The word *fire* was confirmed almost immediately. Others began approaching Jude and telling him that the Lord was going to use him to do something incredible—and each time the only word that they kept hearing was *fire*.

Coincidentally, at the very same time, I was conducting a theological teaching series on the word *fire*—something Jude was completely unaware of. I had just taught on the fiery furnace that the three Hebrew boys were thrown into, as described by King Nebuchadnezzar. I had explained that God is the all-consuming fire—the *fire* that even consumes fire. The Hebrew boys went through the flames, but the fire didn't harm them. They were untouched. There was no trace of it on them—not even the scent of smoke.

God was doing for Jude what He had done for those Hebrew boys.

During this time, Jude was discovering purpose in his pain, and I was gaining clarity on his newfound health. God was speaking loudly to both of us. The all-consuming fire had consumed the "dumpster fire" of Jude's health—and brought with it a promise of great purpose.

Jude never needed a reason or a *why* from God; he needed a purpose for his pain. God responded with just that. Jude has never been the same. I will never forget our final doctor's visit, when the physician looked at us and said, "I have run down all my options. The science is telling me that Jude is healthy."

We walked out, knowing exactly what had happened: God had touched him. The fire of God healed him and revealed his calling. Jude now knew that everything he endured wasn't wasted; it was preparation. His calling is to be a pastor, and he's ready to use his story to minister for the Lord. God's response was better than an answer. God responded by showing Jude his purpose—and it changed everything for him and for us.

I would like to conclude this chapter by praying over you:

> *Lord, I ask for Your loud response to the cry of the one who is hurting so bad from all they have gone through. They need a response from You. You know precisely what they need. You see them right now.*
>
> *Spirit of the living God, reach out to them and bring them clarity. Comfort them, Lord. Comfort them, Lord, in ways they have never been comforted before. Bring them a promise from Your Word. Calm*

*their aching hearts like only You can. Lord, draw
them closer to You in the process. In Jesus' name, amen.*

Finally, I'd like to share a rap song from my son, Jude,
written during the hardest season of his life. He used rap as
a way to pour out his heart before the Lord. This was his
battle cry.

BATTLEGROUND

I've been in the furnace God; I need endurance.
    Fill me with Your strength; I got the table
    turning.
    Hands up, I surrender all my hurting.
I will trust You in the storm cause I know You're
    working.
    God blessed with the flow so I'm still
    discerning,
    I ain't hungry for that fruit; I can see the serpent.
    Put the money in a bag of little boy, you burn it.
    I ain't from this world cause I know the One
    who turn it.

I've been on a battle Opps advancing, started
    shooting round.
    I ain't living for this world already got the crown.
My sword is made out of leather I still cut them
    down.
    I was lost, but all I did was spin around.
Devil hating when we cooking of the Holy sound.
    I know I'm young, but I'm gonna break the
    ground.
I learned to trust even when I couldn't hear a sound.
    It's gonna get tough, but we gonna make it out.

Battleground
Like it's World War III.
I got demons attacking, but I still got peace.
　　Getting knowledge in the storm like it's MIT.
Any demon cross my path, and I'll rest them in peace.
　　Destroying, stealing, killing, you gonna hand
　　　　that to the villain.
You gonna let it slide,
　　Just because you've been up in feelings?
You ain't got no peace cause you've been demon
　　dealing.
　　Satan fishy, he just casted; I can see him reeling.
　　　　　　　　　　　　　　—Jude Miles

Scan this QR code or visit
AutumnMilesBooks.com/
holyghosted/resources to watch
a brief video from me with
encouragement and deeper
insight for your journey.

Chapter 9
THE HOLY BREAKTHROUGH—
WHEN GOD SPEAKS

Then the Lord awoke as if from sleep, like a warrior
overcome by wine. He drove His adversaries back-
ward; He put on them an everlasting reproach.
—PSALM 78:65–66

WHERE IS GOD in the room, Autumn?" the counselor asked. "He's not in the room," I replied.
"You may not be able to find Him, but ask Him
where He is." I sat for several minutes with my head back
on the counselor's comfy, oversized couch, asking the Lord
to show Himself in one of the most traumatic events I had
experienced in my first marriage. The room was getting hot;
my stomach suddenly felt a little queasy. I had felt anxiety
in my spirit all morning, knowing that in my counseling
session that day, we would be covering the abuse that took
place. For years I believed I had healed from those events. I
had helped countless women, churches, couples, teens, and
victims find healing and had been able to move forward in
my own life quite freely as a result. The healing in them
gave my pain a job—a purpose.

But the truth was, not confronting some of the hardest
events had caused reactions and mindsets I didn't even

realize were rooted in unresolved trauma. Because of my lack of awareness, I had unknowingly delayed my own true, Spirit-filled freedom in this specific area of my life for many years. The time had finally come to confront it. It's amazing how Satan will whisper lies in your ear, convincing you that you are healed and that you don't need to do any more work on a particular area—just to keep you as a prisoner of your own memories.

With my eyes closed, I squeezed them tight, forcing myself to see the Lord in that room. The memory of that horrific event had been locked down for several years. It was something that I couldn't forget, but I didn't dare to open Pandora's box to excavate any more information. The truth is, I didn't want to go there. I was fine with never talking about that memory again. I couldn't fully remember many of the memories from that sickening season. I could recall scenes, but my subconscious had blocked the details to protect me.

I adjusted the position I was seated in to accommodate the room's apparent higher temperature. All I could see in my memory was the event itself: the dimness of the room, its layout, and even the bathroom light being on. I felt the sense of evil, my racing heartbeat, and even my fear. It was all coming back to me. I began to recount that moment in detail from the recesses of my mind. But what I couldn't see was God in that room.

My counselor quietly listened as I stumbled through painting a picture that had all but been erased. I squeezed the tissues in my hand, wiping tears that fell rapidly from my squinted eyes as I tried desperately to see God in that room somehow. I confessed, "God wasn't there." How could He be in that horrible room? I couldn't imagine Him being there and not intervening. I was honest. My counselor repeated, "You may not be able to find Him, but, Autumn, He was there." I knew he was right. I know all the Scriptures—I've taught them for years—about how God never leaves us nor forsakes us (Deut. 31:6; Heb. 13:5). Scripture teaches God is omnipresent (Ps. 139:7–8).

When he repeated that line once again, the tears began to flow harder. I realized I'd been angry at God for not intervening. I couldn't understand why He hadn't—and the only way to cope was to assume that He was silent because He wasn't there. The thought that God was there and didn't intervene that horrific day was harder to live with than the thought that He was absent.

Finally, agreeing with my counselor that God must've been in that room allowed me to move forward from the thought that He wasn't. He said, "Take your time. Allow the Holy Spirit to show you where He was." It felt as if I waited for hours. As my head was still leaning back on the couch, I was silent, praying, "God, show me where You were." I waited but nothing happened. Time passed in complete silence.

I held my breath through the tears, anxious to hear from God. This was the moment that needed delicate attention for years, but I had lacked the courage to confront it. This was a holy moment. Nothing mattered except hearing God's voice speak truth into my memory. Nothing.

The air began to shift in the counselor's office. Still intermittently squinting my eyes, I suddenly saw the Lord vividly in the room: His Spirit was above me and slightly behind me. I focused only on Him for a moment.

"I see Him," I whispered, quietly.

My counselor asked, "What is He telling you?"

I felt a rush of emotion seeing God actually present during one of my darkest days. So moved by His posture, I could hardly speak. After years of assuming that He was absent—there He was. Very present. I could barely process my counselor's question, because when God revealed Himself, I was so desperate for it that all my attention was fixed on Him.

With His presence the Lord spoke to me—not with words but with the opportunity to feel what He felt for me. As I gazed at the presence of the Lord, I could see and sense that He watched what was happening to me, and He was angry. I could feel a righteous indignation rise inside me: from Him, for me. I've never sensed something so real in my life. This was new for me.

I remembered Psalm 18—when the Lord was so angry at what was happening to David that He bowed the heavens and came down: "Then the earth shook and quaked; and the foundations of the mountains were trembling and were shaken, because He was angry. Smoke went up out of His nostrils, and fire from his mouth was devouring; coals burned from it" (Ps. 18:7–8, NASB). I knew that verse well and had used it for comfort many times, but in that moment, I knew: God also felt that way for *me*. It was so real, I was deeply moved by the realization that God was not only watching but was angry.

I also vividly perceived that He had abundant compassion for me—the kind of compassion that moves you to act. I remembered when Jesus wept by Lazarus's grave. His compassion was so great that it moved Him. Jesus, many times in Scripture, had compassion for those suffering. I understood that His heart was also breaking for me in that moment—a truth I hadn't considered.

I could also discern in Him a robust sense of justice on my behalf. I was overcome with the sense that God would make all of what I was experiencing right. That stark realization took me by surprise and changed my life. Psalm 37 speaks of the Lord's justice, saying, "The wicked plots against the righteous and gnashes at him with his teeth. The Lord laughs at him for He sees his day is coming" (vv. 12–13).

It was as if He had a yellow legal notepad, taking notes with his ballpoint pen so He could bring harsh justice on my behalf. I knew when I saw Him: He was angry about what happened and overflowing with compassion, knowing I was forced to endure something so horrific. With every fiber of my being, I knew He was already at work to bring justice.

I felt all these feelings simultaneously—even though this event happened more than twenty-four years ago. God was speaking so loudly to me about His involvement and presence that day that I couldn't hear His words—I could only feel Him. What I felt was louder than anything He could say.

My counselor broke my concentration while I was absorbed in that memory. "Autumn, what are you seeing and sensing?"

It was a hard thing to put into words. How do you describe such weighty things with mere words? It seemed like I didn't have any words that would suffice. I slowly, in broken sentences, rattled off a few things I was feeling, but my words could never fully express what my soul felt as my righteous God of justice broke through that day.

The counseling session ended, and as I left, I knew God had finally broken His silence after years of waiting to hear from Him in this area of my life—and that it would change my existence forever. His voice was all I had needed all these years. I just needed to invite His perspective in. I had restricted it for fear of what His voice might reveal. I hadn't wanted to investigate my own memory. But when God finally spoke to me about this incident, His voice healed a very broken place in me—a hidden place that no one, not even I, had been allowed to traverse.

His voice was the balm to my soul. His voice was worth the wait.

Then the Lord Answered

"Then the Lord answered Job out of the whirlwind and said…" (Job 38:1). For thirty-seven chapters of absolute hell on earth, the entire Book of Job has waited with bated breath for this distinguished moment. Heaven, hell, angels, demons, Satan himself, Job, Job's four friends, Job's wife, his staff, the onlookers, the entire supernatural realm, the earthly realm, all creation, and the reader—you and I—have waited, wondered, asked, assumed, and analyzed—all for this one moment: the moment God's silence is broken.

All speeches have been paused. Job and his four friends have come to a point of disagreement where earthly wisdom has ceased. They have nothing left. What they know about God isn't as clear as it once seemed. They all want explanations. Who is right? Where can they point the finger of judgment? Who will God vindicate?

Their theology seems to have failed them. Their theodicy—arguments of how to settle the problem of evil—has collapsed.[1] Wisdom now looks like foolishness, because not one of them can explain the phenomenon of what has been allowed to transpire. No earthly answer exists. The vacuum left by God's silence creates a voracious craving to hear from Him alone.

This is where some of you are right now: You are in the "in-between." Your theology—your study of God—seems to have fallen short of explaining what He has allowed to happen in your life while staying silent.[2] You want more than answers; you want communication from God alone. You don't need to hear another fancy sermon about having more faith or trusting God more; that would only make you nauseous. You simply need to hear His voice.

All earthly explanations have failed and feel inadequate

compared with what you've faced. The melody of His voice is all you yearn for. It is the sound of His voice—no matter what He says—that will bring calm to your soul. You've waited long enough. Let's get into it.

"Then the LORD…" (Job 38:1).

The word *then* is used because when God speaks, it is in response to Job begging to talk with Him and be allowed to argue his case. "But I would speak to the Almighty, and I desire to argue with God" (Job 13:3). Job is allowed all kinds of freedom in this story. He is allowed to question, mourn, wonder, and even assume. God never interrupts Job's words. He has been listening the entire time.

When all is silent—when human wisdom falls short, when Job realizes he doesn't have any idea what was happening, when human logic takes a seat and shuts its mouth—it is *then* that God mercifully and graciously began to respond.

While Job and his friends had waited on God during His silence, God was waiting for them to be silent. Would Job have fully listened if he were too interested in arguing his way before God? Would he have been able to process God's wisdom if he were too caught up in his own? The answer is no. God often waits for us to get silent to break His silence with us.

Sometimes God silences Himself because He waits for you to process yourself into silence.

God's silence—and His delayed response—was mercy. It allowed Job and his friends to analyze themselves out of theological options until they finally had no words left. God was waiting for their silence before He broke His own.

Their silence signaled to God that they were ready to receive from Him. When God sees we are ready to receive, He faithfully responds. God's response gives us insight into what He wants us to know about Himself during our times of questioning.

The first interesting detail is the name used to reference God. The word *Lord* in this verse—"THEN the LORD..."—is the Jewish supreme name for God in Hebrew: *Yahweh* (or *Jehovah*), the same name used during the creation of the world in Genesis.[3] The text tells us that the supreme God—Yahweh, the One who brings all things into existence—is about to respond. Many Hebrew names for God could have been used, but I believe this supreme name was chosen to make a strong point. *Yahweh,* or *Jehovah*, means "He brings into existence whatever exists."[4] So the eternal Creator, Jehovah—the One who holds all power and existence in His hands—is about to speak. That alone asserts His authority without saying a single word. It shifts Job's (and our) perspective, lifting our eyes from the narrow focus of our suffering to the greater reality of God's sovereignty and eternal purpose.

Now that we know Jehovah is answering, it's also important to know *when* He answers. "Then the LORD answered Job out of the whirlwind" (Job 38:1, NKJV). Jehovah is answering Job, not his friends. This is a personal message, just for Job. God responds to *us* personally when we ask. He takes the time to answer us. You are that special to Him. Your pain moves His heart. He knows that you're waiting for His voice, and as previously mentioned, He *will* respond to you.

God decides to answer Job out of the whirlwind. The word *whirlwind* in Hebrew, *sah'-ar,* also means "tempest" and "storm."[5] Jehovah is asserting His power over creation and establishing His authority over Job's personal storm. In a moment of distress, God speaks. He doesn't wait for the storm to pass—He comes in the middle of the whirlwind to speak to Job and calm the storm.

Although this book was written long before the New Testament, it can be seen as a foreshadowing of what Jesus would one day do on earth. In Matthew 14:22–33, we see

Jesus appear in the middle of a storm and command Peter to walk on water. Jesus reveals Himself as the Son of God by asserting His power over the elements—wind, waves, and water—and by addressing the mental strain the storm placed on the disciples. In both accounts—Job in the Old Testament and the disciples in the New Testament—the Trinity makes a clear statement: They are superior to every storm and can calm them all with the sound of their voice. All storms will bow to Jehovah, our Creator—not the other way around. Before Jehovah even utters a word, He communicates His power.

This may have been all Job needed. The way God chose to answer Job—in the whirlwind, showcasing His power—could've been enough to comfort Job. It showed him that God saw, heard what was said, and had come to bring a response. Sometimes all we need is the assurance that God saw and heard what happened. But remember, Job isn't privy to the information that we have. We know from Job 1–2 that Satan, not God, was the one who caused Job's pain. Job, however, isn't sure—he believes God might've caused it. Yet God doesn't just stop at His presence; He offers His words.

GOD'S AUTHORITY BRINGS COMFORT

The first thing God says is, "Who is this that darkens counsel by words without knowledge? Now gird up your loins like a man, and I will ask you, and you instruct Me!" (Job 38:2–3). God immediately begins asking Job questions about creation, using the same divine authority and name attributed to Him in Genesis. He makes a strong statement through a series of rhetorical questions: "Where were you when I laid the foundation of the earth?" (v. 4); "Who enclosed the seas with doors?" (v. 8); "Have you ever in your life commanded the morning?" (v. 12); "Have you entered into the springs of the sea or walked in the recesses of the deep?" (v. 16); "Where is the way to the dwelling of light?" (v. 19); "Do you know the time the mountain goats give birth?" (Job 39:1); and "Do you give the horse his might? Do you clothe his neck with a mane?" (Job 39:19). Shall I go on? I feel like I need to run and hide under a rock. God is making a point. Two whole chapters are filled with questions from God's mouth directly to Job's ear.

This response may seem harsh to a man who has just lost almost everything, but one thing I've realized in my own life—when facing something crushing like Job did—is that the strength of God working on my behalf is more comforting than a hug. It's His strength, ability, and power that calms the storm inside me. The moment I could see God's presence in the incident described at the start of the chapter, peace settled over me. I could sense His feelings toward me; He wouldn't allow evil to endure and would use His power to bring justice. A hug doesn't do that—authority does.

We think we want a hug or a soft word of comfort, and there are a time and a place for those things, but what we really need is to know how mighty our God truly is. The deepest comfort for those of us who've suffered severe trauma isn't found in a well-intentioned word or a temporary embrace; it's the knowledge that our mighty God saw it and that He will exact justice on our behalf. That's true comfort.

EXPAND YOUR HORIZON ON GOD

As previously discussed, God never answers any of Job's questions word for word. Likewise, He doesn't rebuke Job for his raw honesty—even when it seems disrespectful—because He doesn't have to. God does something far more effective than that. He invites Job to a new level of understanding—not focused on Job's pain but centered on God's character. He expands Job's understanding—not on suffering itself but on the nature and ways of God. Job levels up spiritually.

This shift is profound. The process of divine enlightenment that follows educates Job in a realm he hadn't needed access to before his suffering began. But now suffering has extended an exclusive, VIP invitation into a deeper view of who God is and what He is capable of. God never tells Job to deny his feelings—He honors the honesty. But He offers something more powerful than emotional correction: He introduces Job to new information, a new perspective. God doesn't rebuke Job for how he feels; instead, He gently leads him into a new way of thinking. Sometimes our understanding reaches its limit, and it's time for God to advance us to the next grade in the school of Himself.

We will never reach the end of God's wisdom. Romans 11:33 says, "Oh, the depth of the riches both of the wisdom and knowledge of God! How unsearchable are His judgments and unfathomable His ways!" It would be impossible for us to see all the supernatural factors at play during our Job seasons of suffering. Yet suffering becomes a gateway to deeper understanding. You may not gain a new view of God without it. Suffering is often the secret door opened only for those who wrestle to make sense of God's ways. When we walk through that door, God reveals more of Himself—not always to explain everything but to give us a clearer view of His heart, His sovereignty, and His reasoning.

God offers His discourse to Job in two sections. The first, which we've explored, focuses on creation. The second asserts His authority over living creatures. God doesn't just rule creation as a whole; He rules the beings within it. To illustrate, He chooses two rarely mentioned but incredibly powerful examples of His unmatched authority: Behemoth and Leviathan. These so-called "monsters" are described as extremely strong and untamable. God declares that He created Behemoth just as He created Job (Job 40:15), establishing that even the most fearsome creatures are His handiwork. Behemoth is depicted as a massive, powerful land animal—some scholars believe it may be a hippopotamus.[6] In Job 40:24, God asks, "Can anyone capture him when he is on watch, with barbs can anyone pierce his nose?"

Next is the creature Leviathan. In Job 41:1, God asks Job, "Can you draw out Leviathan with a fishhook? Or press down his tongue with a cord?" God continues to describe the terrifying power of this sea-serpent-like monster. In verses 10–11, He declares, "No one is so fierce that he dares to arouse him; who then is he that can stand before Me? Who has given to Me that I should repay him? Whatever is under the whole heaven is Mine." By God's description Leviathan is a fearsome and vicious creature. The Psalms and Isaiah also reference Leviathan, reinforcing its symbolic and literal significance.[7] God even says in verse 33, "Nothing on earth is like him, one made without fear."

You may be asking, "Why are we talking about two monsters? When addressing Job, why would God talk about these two animals?" I'm glad you're wondering—I was too. But think of it this way: If God created and has full control over the most fearsome creatures in nature, what does that say about His power to tame, restrain, and stop the hand of Satan? This National Geographic-like discourse isn't just about animals; it's His way of making a point. If God can subdue the wildest, most powerful beasts, He can certainly overpower the gravest demonic evil without the slightest problem.

God used examples to demonstrate His power to Job in ways Job hadn't even considered. God—if I can put it this way—"dumbed down" His wisdom, making it palatable for

Job. As Job began to grasp the vastness of God's power, his understanding grew.

I want to take a moment and point something out: What you have gone through is real—just as what Job went through was real. What I experienced in the scene I described earlier was very real. The pain and post-traumatic stress disorder (PTSD) it caused has lingered since the day it happened. In some ways I've never been the same. For years I woke up in the middle of the night, gripped by nightmares about the trauma I endured. My breath would be heavy, my heart would race, and my mind would seize with fear and dread. It was only when I received a new perspective from God that my panic attacks began to subside. The nightmares lost their grip, and my anxiety lessened. But for many years those symptoms were very much part of my daily life—because I hadn't yet allowed God to broaden my view of Him.

The feelings we experience from trauma are real, and if we look at God's response to Job, we can see that He doesn't minimize them. You're allowed to feel. God isn't the feelings police. If you are angry with Him, OK. He's big enough to take that anger. Feel what you need to feel, but don't be like me. Don't keep God out of what He wants to heal. I— Ms. Author, Bible teacher, Theology Master's Degree student—kept God out of my trauma. I restricted even Him from accessing the places He longed to make right. If I had let Him in sooner, He would've shown me a side of Himself that took years for me to discover. He would've enlightened my understanding, just as He did Job's. He would've shown me the treasure of His authority and justice that I hadn't even considered. But I kept Him out. While He was trying to invite me into a deeper revelation of who He is, I didn't want to invite Him into my pain.

Maybe this is my plea to you: While I understand how

unspeakably hard it is to process the pain of abuse or sudden tragedy, what you feel isn't the only perspective there is. These kinds of events make people walk away from the faith. They get mad, bitter, and disillusioned. They swear off church or organized religion. They curse God's name, when in truth God didn't cause the evil. God often gets blamed for what He's been longing to redeem. So before you do any of those things—or if you already have—let's restart. Ask God where He was in your trauma. Ask Him how He feels about your heartbreak. Before you go on a full-court press against Him, gently and tenderly ask Him to show you the part of Himself that was present in your suffering—the part you haven't yet seen.

GOD TAKES NOTE OF OUR INJUSTICES

While God didn't interrupt what I went through that day, He took copious notes. His sharp and holy memory remembered everything. Not one emotion—not one detail—of the event was overlooked. All of them were retained. He may not have stepped in to stop what you went through, but friend, He knows everything. He is a God of justice. If you let Him, He will have the final word in your situation.

In my case God has moved so mightily in my life that I'm not the same woman I was back then. He's brought justice for me a thousand times over. Yes, I walked through pain, but nothing compares to the power of watching God have the final word. His appetite for justice far exceeded anything I could've imagined. Where I had let things go, He hadn't. While I had moved on, He stayed until justice was paid in full. Chapter 12 discusses God's justice in a way you may not have heard just yet. I can't wait for you to get there.

That's what happens when we invite God into our deepest

wounds. He does more than comfort—He speaks and confronts them. Ultimately, He has the final say. God's authoritative voice will be heard as He fights for justice on your behalf. Isaiah 30:30 says it like this: "And the LORD will cause His voice of authority to be heard, and the descending of His arm to be seen in fierce anger, and in the flame of a consuming fire in cloudburst, downpour and hailstones."

He is waiting to speak to you, friend. Let Him in. Listen to what He has to say; His words will minister to that deep place of pain inside you.

Scan this QR code or visit AutumnMilesBooks.com/ holyghosted/resources to watch a brief video from me with encouragement and deeper insight for your journey.

Chapter 10
UNHOLY FACTS WITHOUT UNDERSTANDING

Let God be true, and every human being a liar. As
it is written: "So that you may be proved right
when you speak and prevail when you judge."
—ROMANS 3:4, NIV

I s THIS WHAT being madly in love feels like?" I thought as I wiped the beaded sweat from my forehead. I was sitting in the third row from the back of a makeshift tent–auditorium that was outside in the elements of an old campground. It was hot and humid, and even though the sun had set, the heat hadn't subsided.

I was surrounded by at least twenty-five middle school girls and about the same number of high school girls. I was the only female youth intern the church I was working for had ever dared to hire. They took a risk on me, and as the only one, I was deemed the leader of all things *girl* for the entire youth group, which included being the lead camp counselor for the summer camp that we were attending.

That summer I was their leader. We were having the time of our lives. I was obsessed with each of them. With my divorce behind me and a new lease on life, I poured my heart into these precious girls.

If they wanted me to eat raw food, I did. If they wanted me to dress up like a clown for the camp challenge to earn team points, I did. If they wanted me to see whether the guy they liked also had a crush on them, I was their designated wingman. If they needed some good old-fashioned correction, I gave it. If they needed a good scolding, I was their girl. If they needed prayer, I stopped everything I was doing and prayed. If they needed counsel, I was their go-to.

Everything I did, I took a group of youth group girls with me. We had ice cream and coffee dates, mall runs, and nail appointments—we did it all. I loved every minute, and even now I miss those days.

They were my people. I am still a girl's girl.

One of the things we did that summer was go to Ohio's best-known amusement park, Cedar Point. My boyfriend (at the time), Eddie Miles, had made the trip to Ohio to visit me and joined us for the outing.

The girls roasted me as I walked around the park with him that day, smiling and making googly eyes at each other. We looked like the classic picture of true love—so much so that we were annoying to watch—like, really annoying. We were nauseating to watch, so I understood why they couldn't help themselves and made fun of me so much.

I didn't care, because Eddie and I were at the point where our relationship was changing rapidly from "like" to love. I was beginning to lose sight of where I ended and where he began. God kept confirming my relationship with him almost daily. Things were heating up fast, and on that warm, humid camp night—even though I was supposed to be engaged as a good church staffer should be—he was all I could think about.

One of the camp staffers took the stage and announced that the regular camp speaker had a family emergency;

therefore, a new guy would be speaking henceforth. The new guy walked on the stage. He was very young and was probably around my age at the time, twenty-three years old. He was green, but if you heard him talk, you would think he had God completely figured out.

I turned my nose up as I listened, because he was constantly referring to himself. I thought, "Hmm, this guy thinks *a lot* of himself." With that thought I turned my attention back to Eddie and wondered whether this was who God wanted me to marry.

Could God really be setting me up with a blessing like Eddie? Is God *really* that good? I wondered whether he was all he seemed to be. Surely, he had a flaw somewhere. He was so hot, and he loved Jesus so much. Score!

I began to thank God for our relationship and how much it contrasted with the marriage He had delivered me from a few years before. I hadn't experienced love, so this was new to me.

The new guest speaker began winding down, so I reluctantly turned my attention back to the message, because I knew that I would be responsible for leading the spiritual group discussion with my girls later. As the speaker began his altar call, he glanced in my direction and made eye contact with me. I quickly looked away; it felt awkward. A few seconds later, as I half-listened to what he was saying, he looked directly at me again. Feeling the awkwardness intensify, and still unsure how he could even see me from all the way in the back, I glanced away once more.

The service finally ended with a closing prayer. I grabbed all my belongings and gave the girls quick instructions to meet me outside by the firepit. When I turned around, I noticed the guest speaker walking toward me, staring me down as he approached. He had some speed in his step, and I didn't know whether I should run the other way or wait to see what he had to say. I decided to wait. He walked right up to me and introduced himself. Respectfully, I did the same.

He began making small talk, asking me why I was at youth camp and what my role was. He was spitting out questions so quickly, I could tell he was a little nervous. Finally, after what felt like enough small talk, I gently interrupted and said, "I'm so sorry, but I have to lead the message discussion with my girls." He quickly responded, "Can we talk after that?" I said sure, not thinking much about it, and off I went.

He came and found me as soon as our discussion time had concluded. It was like he had been watching from afar. This time he brought an entourage with him. My girls were all gathered around me while he struck up a new conversation. Our back-and-forth banter was fun for them to watch. As I was about to tell him I needed to take the girls to their cabins for lights out, he bravely—and very vulnerably—declared, "Can we go on a date?" Everyone froze. Silence. No one said a word. No one quite knew how to respond to the sudden question, least of all me.

I stumbled for words, as my mind was still full of daydreams about Eddie during the guest speaker's entire message. I said something like, "Uhhh, well, that is so nice of you to ask. I'm honored..." Before I could even finish my answer, he blurted out, this time with full authority and confidence, "God told me that you are my wife." More silence. More bewilderment. Every bystander was stunned. The statement caught me so off guard that I didn't even respond at first. The audacity of this guy. Who does that? I mean, that is quite a statement. His wife? He didn't know me. He just told me, straight up, "God told me that you are my wife." Really? We had just met. What if I was an axe murderer? How was he supposed to know that? The girls around me seemed to take a collective step back, wide-eyed at the brazen declaration. All their eyes locked on me, waiting to see what in the world I would say.

So much was going on in my head that this young man didn't know. He didn't know I had been divorced. He didn't know that God had redeemed my life from hell. He didn't know my personality, didn't know that I was seriously dating my now-husband, and didn't know that I had just been asking God in prayer if this is what love felt like. This bold, young, arrogant man spoke without knowing any of those things. He declared a statement about God and me without knowing the facts.

I had no intention of humiliating this guy. Maybe he *did* think God had told him that. Maybe he felt a nudge from the Holy Ghost. Maybe he was genuinely convinced. But I didn't feel the same. In fact, I felt quite the opposite. I took a second to gather my thoughts before responding. I looked him in the eyes and said as kindly as I possibly could, "God didn't tell me that. I am so sorry, but God hasn't revealed that to me." I didn't know what else to say. How could I agree with him when I already knew where God was leading me? I couldn't. I wouldn't. He had declared that which he knew nothing about. He got this one wrong.

I don't remember what he said after that—just his look. It seemed as if he was offended that I, as a woman, had the audacity to hear from God. (Yikes.) We wouldn't have made a good match at all. With my girls in tow, I remember slowly turning and walking away. One of them whispered, "Wow, that took a lot of guts." Another asked, "Did he really hear that from God?" One giggled and said, "He was cute." Another chimed in: "I can't believe you dropped him like that."

I paused, knowing this was a teachable moment. "Girls," I said, "if God says something about you to someone else,

He'll also confirm it to you. That young man didn't hear from God. He spoke first without understanding my situation." We ended up having an entire conversation about being careful when making declarations about God without having all the facts. To this day I still use that moment as an example of someone who spoke out of turn using God's name.

DECLARATIONS WITHOUT KNOWLEDGE

Why do I use this example? Because chances are, we've all been that young youth pastor at some point. I know I've done that exact thing: spoken boldly and declaratively about something I knew nothing or little about. I've even done it about God. You probably have too. That's why this chapter matters.

The young youth pastor did it. Most of us are guilty of speaking declaratively without having all the facts. Our boy Job did it too. He was confident in what he thought he knew about God. As previously discussed, he made assumptions, asked hard questions, and made bold declarations, but he didn't have the whole story. He hadn't yet reached a new level of understanding. The following are a few of Job's more shocking claims about God: Job declared that God was his enemy (Job 13:24); he claimed that "he laughs at the death of the innocent" (Job 9:23, NLT) and that God "smile[s] on the counsel of the wicked" (Job 10:3, NKJV); and he believed that God was angry with him (Job 19:7–27). Was Job malicious or disrespectful? No, he was just deeply wounded and didn't yet fully understand who God actually was.

I've been there. I've said things like, "God must be done with me," "God's mad at me," and "God isn't going to help me this time." I've made those declarations and probably a thousand more. Like Job, they weren't rooted in truth; they were the outcry of a girl who just didn't yet understand the fullness of who God is.

I want to break down Job's response to God breaking His silence.

In the previous chapter, we unpacked how Jehovah finally spoke. The entire book seemed desperate for His voice—for Jehovah's authority to step in. When God did, everything shifted.

Suddenly, Job had a change of tune. The man who once wanted to argue his case before God now backed down (Job 13:3). He stood nearly speechless at God's response—dumbfounded by how little he truly knew, simply by standing in the presence of the author of knowledge.

Job 42:2–3 begins his humble response. Imagine Job—probably hesitant to speak a single word—saying, "I know You can do all things, and that no purpose of Yours can be thwarted (stopped). 'Who is this that hides counsel without knowledge?' Therefore I have declared that which I did not understand, things too wonderful for me, which I did not know."

Rather than getting his long-awaited questions answered—a demand that once consumed him—Job was flabbergasted. God had left him speechless. Encountering God made him realize there are infinite facets to God—realities he had never considered. God had allowed him to speak freely, to vent his grief, and to ask every question on his mind. But now freshly introduced to a new side of the Almighty, Job sees it as beneath both God and his new understanding to continue in such self-absorbed interrogation.

This new side of God left Job in verbal paralysis. In his deep grief, the revelation acted as a healing balm. His heart still ached, his body still suffered, and his mind was still tired from exhaustion, but a brand-new glimpse of who

God truly is calmed those severe ailments and rendered him nearly speechless. Rather than cursing God to His face, Job recognized where the error lay: in his own lack of knowledge of how wonderful and truly majestic the God he had questioned really was. Job's judgments about God had been based on a side of God he had never known before.

I want to pause and humbly check in with you. Friend, the freedom to ask questions—or to be brutally honest—with God is a beautiful gift He mercifully gives us. But hear this from your sister: What God wants to reveal to you through what you've faced will change you and inspire you far more than simply getting all the answers. Take it from Job—your soul will find deeper satisfaction in a new measure of God, gained through this trial, than in any explanation you could receive. I know that's hard to believe, but God is that holy. This very season you're walking through holds the golden ticket to a richer, more robust knowledge of Him.

Job's response spoke of God's purpose—specifically, that no purpose of His can be thwarted or stopped (Job 42:2). I submit that, in the revelations God gave Job, he couldn't help but recognize the purpose behind what God described in Job 38–41. The God who mastered mysterious creatures such as the Behemoth and Leviathan could also master and assign purpose to the mysterious trials in Job's life.

My friend, the same is true for you. Purpose exists for what you're facing right now. In some of my harshest trials, I've had to wait to see it unfold—but the moment a trial began, God had already assigned it a purpose.

When Eddie and I were waiting to adopt, a woman scammed us by pretending she was pregnant with twin girls. It wasn't our adoption agency who uncovered the truth—it was the Holy Spirit who revealed it. As soon as we were matched, I had an unease in my spirit. A lack of peace began to plague me about this particular woman. After many questions and phone calls, the lack of peace got worse. It became full-blown anxiety. That lack of peace drove me to do an investigation of sorts. The Holy Spirit led me to information, exposing that this woman wasn't even pregnant. She was scamming us, and we were devastated. As angry as I was, I had walked with the Lord long enough to know that—as painful as it is to be lied to, betrayed, and have money stolen—there was purpose in it. God never wastes anything.

Until then, adopting one child was all we had ever considered; two more children weren't in the plan. After all, we already had two biological children, Grace and Jude. But saying yes to those "twins"—though they didn't exist— opened our hearts in a way we hadn't expected. It showed us we wanted to adopt two, not just one.

Two years later, when our adoption agency presented Moses to us, our answer was an immediate yes. The very next day, when Haven was offered, we said yes again without hesitation. Looking back, I realize we might never have known our hearts were open to more than one child if God hadn't revealed it through that earlier experience. I shudder to think of a life without both Moses and Haven—we were meant to be their parents.

Had God not allowed us to walk through the horrible scam, we may never have been open to two of the most incredible blessings I've ever known. He allowed a short-term hurt for long-term joy. Friend, there is a purpose for you too—even if you can't see it yet.

Is God Allowed to Question You?

In Job's response he actually answers a question God asked him. After thirty-eight chapters of Job's own questions and assumptions, God had some questions of His own. God asks Job, "Who is this that darkens counsel by words without knowledge? Now gird up your loins like a man, and I will ask you, and you instruct Me!" (Job 38:2–3). (Yikes.) But Job, in his humility, responds. He repeats God's question and then—in the Autumn Miles translation—essentially says, "It was me. I take full responsibility, and I didn't know what I was talking about."

We're quick to question God when all hell breaks loose, but do we allow Him to question us? Is it a two-way street?

Let me ask you as your friend: Is God allowed to ask, "Why have you stayed away from talking to Me for so long?" or, "Why don't you want anything to do with Me anymore?" or, "Are you bitter about something I can help with?"

In the Garden of Eden, God asks Adam and Eve, "Where are you?" (Gen. 3:9). Can He question you? Can His Word question you? Will you allow His Word to hold you accountable for your thoughts?" Can He ask, "Why are you angry, and why have you given up? If you let Him, sweet friend, He just might give a new perspective—one that changes your life entirely, just as He did for Job.

THE WORD OF GOD DID THE WORK

When we allow the Lord to ask us questions—and let His Word challenge us rather than offend us—it works within us. It snatches victory right from the enemy's hands. The open dialogue we see in Job—his raw questions met by God's authoritative responses—breeds understanding that strengthens faith rather than weakens it.

Those who fall away from faith in harsh trials usually lack one of two things: Either they never asked their questions, or they never allowed God the opportunity to respond. Some shut off their minds to Him early in the trial; others shut off their hearts when His answer seems delayed.

The discourse in Job, though treacherous to read, gives us a healthy communication model with God—one that builds faith rather than extinguishes it. This is what our Christian life should be like. When we let the Word of God work in us, it will do exactly what He sent it to do. It produces more faith in Him, not less—if we surrender and let it do its work. As Isaiah 55:11 (NIV) declares, "So is My word that goes out from My mouth: It will not return to me empty, but will accomplish what I desire and achieve the purpose for which I sent it."

These trials had a purpose: to give Job a brand-new perspective on who God is. That was their holy purpose. The process was full of rough and sometimes messy dialogue, but it was what Job needed to get there.

THIS IS WHERE SATAN LOST

Satan was never after Job's stuff. He wasn't even ultimately after Job. He was after Job's faith. Until God spoke, Satan still had a chance at the most precious jewel he could never steal—Job's faith. However, he could only take his faith if Job surrendered it. Though Satan is a thief, he can't steal faith unless it's given.

Faith is one of the only things that must be handed over to him. He fought hard to secure a victory for himself and the forces of evil. If he could get Job to renounce his faith—after the whole East knew him for it—he would gloat over the victory for generations. I'm sure he waited and wondered how it would turn out. He saw Job cry, suffer, ask endless questions, and come dangerously close to giving up on the things of God. Job's pain was excruciating, but even stronger than his pain was the rock on which his faith was built.

When God spoke, it was over for the enemy. When God speaks, the enemy loses. He has to retreat like the fool he is. Nothing is stronger than a man or woman whom God allows into the secret place of His majesty. No pain is worth forfeiting the glory God has just revealed. God's Word sealed Job's victory.

You see, where Satan thought he had a chance, God knew—before the attack ever began—that he had none. God saw the depth of Job's faith and knew that one word from the Great Shepherd would bring him back home. God baited the great baiter himself, Satan, and He won. While Satan is crafty and the ultimate deceiver, God is faithful and true. When God spoke truth, the refreshing presence of its freedom changed Job's life and perspective. One word from the Lord will change your life too. Satan never had a chance. Job's faith remained because his understanding of God increased. It turns out faith in God can withstand the loss of everything: health, wealth, children, friends, and even mental health.

Though pressing, suffering and loss can't crush it all together. It's what Paul declared in 2 Corinthians 4:8–9, "We are afflicted in every way, but not crushed; perplexed, but not despairing; persecuted, but not forsaken; struck down, but not destroyed." When trials hit, someone whose feet are firmly planted on the bedrock of God Himself will always rise and be refreshed the moment they hear His voice.

Little did Satan know—it was *because* of the affliction that Job's faith became stronger. In trying to destroy Job, Satan unwittingly created a faith machine. He helped build Job's faith—not weaken it. Loss, even when severe, is no match for faith—no matter how small—when it is rooted in the Master of the universe.

The Book of Job shows us that even weak, feeble faith can endure even great loss. That's how unshakable faith in God truly is. Satan lost because God outwitted him. The enemy's intelligence is limited, just as Job's was. He didn't see that outcome coming—or he likely would've left Job alone. But God saw it all in advance, and He tricked the great trickster.

NOW MY EYES SEE YOU

"I have heard of You by the hearing of the ear, but now my eye sees You" (Job 42:5). This is one of my favorite verses in the entire Book of Job. It is a brand-new declaration—a declaration spoken with understanding. Job finally *gets it*.

Until now, he had been taught about God by what he heard but not through what he had personally seen for himself. That changed instantly. He held on until the end and received the greatest prize: a revelation of God's majesty. He gained a new level of faith and a deeper understanding of God's goodness.

Job was seeing something he had lived his whole life without. He might've been content not "seeing" this new side of God, but God wasn't content leaving him there. God loved Job enough to introduce him to something spectacular about Himself.

Now Job could declare with knowledge—where before, he had spoken without understanding.

Friend, while there are many reasons God allows trials, I believe this is one of the most beautiful: When the pressing brings us to our knees—asking, seeking, desperately clinging to Jesus—He can reveal a part of Himself we wouldn't have known before.

No other friend to my faith has been greater than trials. They *could* have slaughtered my faith—but instead, surrender saved it. When I've said, "God I don't like this. I don't understand this. But I am sticking with You, because there is no hope in anything else," I've opened the door for God to take me deeper.

Every time I've surrendered during a trial, I've come out with a higher level of personal understanding of who He is.

After my divorce—when I lost everything and almost every friend I had ever known—I discovered that all I truly needed was God. He was sufficient. When everything else was stripped away, I learned that He alone was enough for me to survive. It was His provision that put my life back together.

That season taught me something I'll never forget: When your life looks demolished—when it seems like it can't be salvaged—with God, it can always be restored. Restoration is always possible.

Years later, when the Holy Spirit revealed that we were being scammed by a birth mother who claimed she was pregnant with twin girls, and when we uncovered the falsified documents, I thought, "How in the world will God work this out?" The hurt, betrayal, and loss felt too deep.

But a year and a half later, on a Wednesday, we received a call: A baby boy needed a home, and his birth mother had chosen us. The very next day we received another call: A little girl needed a home, and her birth mother chose us too. We said yes to both without hesitation.

God restored our twins.

My mind already *knew* God was capable of these things, but now my eyes *saw* Him do it. I saw Him on a higher level than ever before—in a new dimension. With each blow that comes through trials, this is one of the rewards He lavishes His children with: a deeper, more personal revelation of Himself. You can't buy this kind of faith; you earn it by pressing into Him through the trial.

My sweet friend, these words may fall on deaf ears right now. Or maybe you are sitting on the edge of your seat, bawling into a tattered tissue way past its prime because you want so badly to believe this—yet it's hard to hope again. Whatever the case, the reward remains. Purpose will spring forth from what you've had to endure if you cling to the Master's hand, even if it's only by the pinkie finger.

A new day will dawn, bringing with it a fresh, striking view of God that will minister to your grief. Your eyes will see Him for yourself; you'll never again have to rely only on someone else's story or faith. You can speak with authority, like Job: "I have heard of You by the hearing of the ear, but now my eye sees You."

You, the student, will become a teacher for those who suffer after you. You can speak with the same certainty Job had, and the comfort you've received from what you've seen will offer others the strength they need to persevere.

The following are some verses to meditate on as we close this chapter:

> Blessed is the man who remains steadfast under trials, for when he has stood the test he will receive the crown of life, which God has promised to those who love him.
>
> —James 1:12, esv

> Do you not know that in a race all the runners run, but only one receives the prize? So run that you may obtain it.
>
> —1 Corinthians 9:24, esv

Not only that, but we rejoice in our sufferings knowing that suffering produces endurance, and endurance produces character, and character produces hope.

—Romans 5:3–4, esv

Count it all joy, my brothers, when you meet trials of various kinds, for you know that the testing of your faith produces steadfastness. And let steadfastness have its full effect, that you may be perfect and complete, lacking in nothing.

—James 1:2–4, esv

Scan this QR code or visit AutumnMilesBooks.com/holyghosted/resources to watch a brief video from me with encouragement and deeper insight for your journey.

Chapter 11
HOLY REPENTANCE

He who conceals his transgressions will not prosper, but he who confesses and forsakes them will find compassion.
—PROVERBS 28:13

SEVERAL YEARS AGO, on a rainy afternoon, I was running to my car when my phone rang. I was rushing around to wrap up the last few Easter tasks. In our home Easter is a huge deal. I've committed to celebrating Easter the way we celebrate Christmas—and naturally, that means wearing myself out with all the various traditions I've decided are important.

This year was no different. I was busy picking out new outfits for the six of us, gathering ingredients for Easter dinner, booking nail and hair appointments for everyone. The prep was intense, but I enjoyed every minute of it. At that moment I was leaving a popular Dallas tanning salon, fresh from my golden Easter spray tan.

Not wanting the rain to ruin my fresh glow, I let the call go to voicemail. As soon as I was safe and dry in the car, I looked to see who had called. It was my mom. Sheltered from the artillery of the rain, I called her back. She answered, with a shaky voice, "Autumn, how are you, sugar?"

"Sugar" is what she's called us kids for as long as I can remember. While I'm not sure of its origin, I know this:

When she says it, something serious is on her mind. She uses this word before sharing hard medical news about my dad or delivering unexpected changes to our plans.

Answering her question just to appease her, I rattled off about my day, fully aware her mind was on other matters. When I finished my quick recap, I asked, "Mom, what's up?" She paused. "Well, how are you?" she asked again. Her question still felt off—I had just answered it. "Mom, I'm fine. What is going on?"

"You are? You're fine?" she pressed.

"Yes, Mom. Why are you being so weird?"

"Autumn, have you checked your email?"

"No, I haven't."

"Check it," she replied.

I sat in my car as rain pelted the windshield, the wipers keeping frantic time with the pounding in my chest. As quickly as humanly possible, I switched Mom to speakerphone and opened my inbox. She was right—a fresh email had arrived. Nothing could've prepared me for the name staring back at me: a familiar, unwelcome one—a blast from my past.

Honestly, it was a name I had hoped never to hear—or see—again in my lifetime. I had counted on eternity to judge it according to my memory of this person. I was immediately triggered. My pulse quickened. I hesitated, unwilling to open the email. That name carried some of the darkest days of my life—one of the greatest betrayals I had ever endured. When I needed the church most, the entire deacon board at my dad's church—where I grew up—kicked me out. I had already moved on, and God had done a miraculous work of healing in me. But that day the memory alone sent a shiver down my spine.

With my mom—and now my dad—on speakerphone, I

clicked to open the email. I have to admit: It took courage to read the email instead of just deleting it and sending it straight to the cyber trash can. What can you do when an enemy from your past suddenly decides—right in the middle of buying Easter candy for your kids' Easter baskets—that *now* is the time to talk?

So many thoughts consumed me as I stared at the email, weighing the emotional consequences of even reading it. But I felt the Holy Spirit prod me with a quiet comfort, as if to say, "It's OK. Open it."

So I did.

My parents silently waited on the line as I began reading the email from someone who had caused some of the deepest pain in my life. The moment my eyes scanned the first sentence, I froze. My heart began to race, outpacing even the windshield wipers still swiping away the rain. My anxiety spiked to a ten. I knew instantly—this was an apology email.

I was shocked. I had long since given up any expectation of an apology, or even an acknowledgment of wrongdoing from those who had kicked me out of my home church when I needed them most. I didn't think I needed it anymore. I had moved on. I had forgiven them. I had chosen to forgive every single person involved, never waiting for an apology. One day I had even spoken their names aloud and said, "I forgive you."

This email was the kind of thing I had once longed for. Back then, I would've given anything for someone to say, "Hey, I'm sorry we kicked you out of the church your dad pastored. Maybe we could've done something biblical—like help you, especially because you were being abused. Sorry for ruining your life." But that apology never came. Because it never happened, I had to learn how to forgive without being asked for it.

In fact, I had grown thankful for every person involved.

Their actions had given me the chance to be pastored directly by the Holy Spirit—to discover how He personally leads when human leaders fail. Because of that heartbreak and utter betrayal, God opened a door for me to minister to millions of people over the years who had experienced the same kind of pain. What Satan meant for evil, God used for good.

I didn't need an apology letter from anyone—but there it was, staring back at me from my screen. Without me asking, God had given it to me.

I read the letter in a state of shock. Immediately, I burst into tears—not because of the details but because of the spirit in which it was written. Humility saturated every line. Each sentence seemed to drip with the sweet essence of repentance. I had never known some of the facts it contained, but the email brought clarity to questions I had carried for years. It gave context. It revealed some of the calculated, even salacious, plans of the individuals involved. More than anything, it offered a heartfelt, sincere, and beautifully precious apology for the betrayal itself. One line, in particular, gripped me: "I repent with dust and ashes." You can't get humbler than that.

As I finished reading the letter, a sweet spirit of gratitude swelled in my car. With my parents still on the phone, the three of us sat together in silence for a while. I had no idea what to say. This was a gift that couldn't be bought—a balm for the soul that no prescription could ever offer. It filled me with unexpected joy. I hadn't thought I needed it, but somehow it reached deep places in me that were quietly healed at that moment.

My voice cracked as I finally spoke. I think I said something like, "Wow... I don't even know what to say. That was incredibly kind." My parents, knowing the tremendous pain I went through, were deeply moved as well. That day

I realized the importance of true repentance. It changes the posture of the one who repents and changes the posture of the one who receives it. Repentance restores something that can never fully be restored if that step is skipped. It breathes new life. It brings relief. It ushers a new sense of freedom for both parties. Grace takes a seat at the table, and a repentant heart eats its fruit. The value of that moment was immeasurable. Its value alone was supernatural. Repentance is one of the greatest blessings that we can participate in. It changes everything.

That day something shifted in me. An egregious evil once perpetrated against me somehow became a blessing. The shell around a dormant piece of my heart finally cracked open. On top of that beautiful show of humility, the dead places betrayal had killed in me came to life again. True repentance did that. I wanted to shout. I wanted to cry. I wanted to give this man—a man absolutely courageous, humble, and clearly under deep conviction—a hug. God had already blessed me through the betrayal, but now He was ushering in a fresh gift of peace about a situation I had long endured without an apology. A year earlier, I might've said this letter was long overdue—but that day I realized it was right on time.

REPENTANCE IS A GIFT THAT IS UNDERUTILIZED

Believers often underutilize repentance—myself included. It is one of the greatest gifts for emotional and mental freedom that God has given us, yet we treat it as a last resort. Sometimes we don't need a pill or a therapy session. Sometimes we just need repentance.

Satan wants it that way—he doesn't want you to repent. He wants you trapped by bottled-up anxiety and lingering regret over your wrongdoings. He knows repentance will set you free, so he offers a substitute instead. He gives you something to keep you busy and distracted, so you'll choose the counterfeit over the one thing that will bring true emotional healing: repentance.

The substitute of the hour is deflection. As believers, we have embraced it—shifting the focus to someone or something else rather than taking responsibility for the part we may have played. If we've experienced "church hurt," we often claim it's always the church's fault. But the truth is, it's not *always* the church's fault. Sometimes another person simply tried to hold us accountable. (I can speak with authority on this one, considering I was kicked out of church.) In other situations, it's always "their" fault. While, yes, maybe most of it *was* the other party's fault—are we sure we played no part in it at all?

We have picked up deflection as a way to mask our wrongdoing instead of facing the truth: Sometimes we are wrong. In those moments, we can't place blame anywhere else but on ourselves. After all, if it's always "their" fault, it can't be ours—right? Deflection is a cheap counterfeit for repentance. It's easier to process. It may temporarily free us emotionally from guilt or conviction. But make no mistake: Deflection is *not* a substitute for repentance. Nothing is. It will never produce the same result.

The enemy wants us to deflect rather than repent. He wants the blame to stay on someone else, so we never live in righteousness. After all, isn't he called the accuser of the brethren? (Rev. 12:10). If we accuse "them" without ever acknowledging our own part, aren't we doing exactly what he does?

We need to return to the practice of coming before the

Lord, asking where we have erred and repenting. There is no substitute for walking before Him with a clean heart.

REPENTANCE BRINGS JOY

Satan often paints repentance as unnecessary. We've widely accepted repentance for our eternal life. Scripture makes that clear. (See 1 John 1:9; Ps. 51:10.) But what about repentance for our daily lives? We say, "Repent from your sin, or you will go to hell." But do we ever say, "Repent often from the sins you commit throughout your life, or you will live in an emotional state of hell?" No, we don't, because it isn't flashy. It doesn't preach well. Our flesh craves the fluff, not the facts.

I've written about repentance before, but the Lord has really deepened my understanding of its value. I've realized that repentance is often the quickest way back to joy. A while back, I found myself living in a constant state of frustration. Nothing seemed to bring me joy. I would sit with the Lord, read His Word, and I still couldn't find joy. I knew joy was possible; I'm a joyful person by nature. But I felt heavy inside.

Eddie and I faced circumstances beyond our control, making me so frustrated and angry. One morning, while I was with the Lord, I felt Him gently prod my heart: "You can't change them, but you can walk before Me with a clean heart." Immediately, I knew I needed to stop focusing on what was being done to us and start focusing on my posture before the Lord.

So I began to evaluate my heart. Was I sinless in this situation? No, I had said things I shouldn't have, carried a horrible attitude for what seemed like ages, complained constantly, and harbored judgment toward those who had caused the problem. The whole thing was just all-around icky. I hadn't caused the situation, but I *was* still responsible for how I chose to walk through it.

I sat in prayer and began calling out my wrong attitudes one by one: my complaining spirit, my self-pity, my harsh words, and my judgment. I said the words aloud: "I repent. Please forgive me." With each confessed sin, I felt lighter inside. By the time I was finished, I felt like a new person.

I realized I had been so caught up in *deflection* that I had missed the real way for joy to return: repentance. That day I walked differently. The things that had made me angry seemed to just roll right off my back. My joy returned. I had a pep in my step—not because the problem disappeared, but because my posture before the Lord had changed.

From then on, I began starting my quiet time with repentance. I noticed my challenges felt smaller when my heart was right as I walked through them. I didn't just regain joy; I discovered a *deeper* joy. Repentance made the difference. Repentance brought me back to joy.

REPENTANCE EASED JOB

After God speaks, one of the most profound verses in Job is his repentance: "Therefore I retract, and I repent, sitting on dust and ashes" (Job 42:6, NASB). The Hebrew word used for "repent" is *nāham*, which means "to comfort or repent," but it can also mean "to comfort oneself or ease oneself."[1]

Job needed relief from something. Earlier we read, "Despite all this, Job did not sin" (Job 1:22, NASB). After hearing directly from the Lord, however, it's clear Job is convicted that he has erred in some way. Maybe it was the new depth of knowledge from God that he had just gained. Maybe he realized he had been too harsh. Maybe he felt the sting of conviction for accusing God.

What's fascinating is that God never demanded Job's repentance, yet Job still offered it. He *chose* to repent, to "ease himself," simply because he knew in his heart that he needed to.

Repentance does that. It eases you. As previously shared, I've never repented for anything without immediately feeling my spirit grow lighter. That day Job was finally at peace with himself.

He goes further, saying, "I repent in dust and ashes." The significance of this statement can't be missed. These were the exact words the person used in the letter: "I repent with dust and ashes." But why this wording? Dust and ashes are symbols of grief and humility. Dust points to our nothingness and to our deep humility before God, while ashes represent sorrow and repentance.

Although God didn't ask Job to repent, Job felt compelled to do so, acting with a profound sense of humility. From the start Job had lived with a humble posture before the Lord (Job 1). But now he saw God in a new light and felt the need to bow even lower under His mighty hand. "Humble yourselves under the mighty hand of God, so that He may exalt you at the proper time" (1 Pet. 5:6, NASB). Job did just that, and he was eased.

REPENTANCE PLEASED GOD

It was directly after Job repented before the Lord that God began to judge those who had wronged him and set in motion the blessings that followed. Job's posture before the Lord pleased God. Though Job wasn't responsible for the tragedies that had struck his life, he was responsible for how he responded to them. I believe that, because Job humbled himself and made his heart right before God, He chose to bless Job abundantly.

Listen, I won't pretend to understand the depths of God's thoughts or emotions when we repent and confess our sin on a regular basis. How could I? No one knows God's mind (1 Cor. 2:11). But I do know how I felt when the man from my past—without my asking—asked for forgiveness. I felt a rush of joy and a sense of alignment. In an instant the barrier between us was gone. There was no longer "me" and "him." There was just us. Unity filled the space. If he called me today, I would answer. If I saw him on the street, I would give him a hug. Repentance had built a bridge between us in a single moment.

I often think about this from God's perspective. We may not always be carrying some deep, glaring sin that demands repentance, but what about the smaller ones—the ones so subtle we dismiss them or the ones we deflect rather than own? Those hidden things build a chasm between us and God, and the only way across is through confession, repentance, and receiving His forgiveness.

While I can't claim to know exactly what God thinks, I do know this: It pleases Him. Unity is restored when we repent. Heaven rejoices when even one sinner repents (Luke 15:7). I believe that, from the supernatural side, our daily acknowledgment of sin and turning back to God brings Him the same delight. Repeatedly, Scripture shows God intervening when Israel turns from idols and returns to Him. If this happens on a national scale, imagine the joy it brings to His heart when His children do it daily.

Repentance is for you and for God. It eases you, and it pleases Him. I wrote this chapter after finishing the entire manuscript. I had already turned it in when, the week before my deadline, the Lord spoke to my heart: "I don't want a paragraph on repentance; I want an entire chapter." When

I met with my publisher, they generously agreed I should write it and send it in.

I believe this message is straight from the heart of God. Repentance isn't offered nearly as often as it should be. Yes, repentance gets us into heaven, but daily repentance allows us to live a piece of heaven on earth.

I feel like I'm letting you in on a secret. Some of you simply need to sit with the Lord, evaluate yourself before Him, and repent as the Holy Spirit brings to mind any sin you may have overlooked. The secret to the joy you've been longing for is found in His presence with a clean heart before Him. When your heart is clear, joy is unleashed. You now have the opportunity to be "eased" in your spirit.

This chapter is shorter than the others, but perhaps it's the most important. Take some time now, my love, to sit before Him in repentance. Joy is waiting.

 Scan this QR code or visit AutumnMilesBooks.com/ holyghosted/resources to watch a brief video from me with encouragement and deeper insight for your journey.

Chapter 12
HOLY JUSTICE FOR YOU—
GOD WANTS TO TAKE CARE
OF JUSTICE FOR YOU

For the LORD *loves justice and does not forsake His godly ones; they are preserved forever, but
the descendants of the wicked will be cut off.*
—PSALM 37:28

THE AIR WAS fresh that April evening as I hurried toward my black Jeep Cherokee, breathing rapidly and fighting what felt like the onset of a panic attack. As I approached my car, my childhood flashed through my mind like an old film reel. This same blacktop parking lot—its sealant sharp in the cool night air—had once been the playground of my spring, summer, and fall evenings. I had walked it every Sunday, morning and evening, to the church my father pastored throughout my youth. I played tag, sang old '90s country songs with the youth group, found my first church crush, and waved to countless people coming and going.

There were dark purple snow cones after Sunday night service, the aroma of Wednesday night fellowship dinners, and the thrill of learning to drive. All those memories ambushed me as I rushed to my car that night, which felt like an unfair advantage. The diagonally painted, bright yellow lines marking the parking spaces now felt like a tally of moments gathered over the past twenty-two years. I fumbled for my keys to unlock the door to my "chariot" that would take me away as fast as possible, but the memories—coupled with the three-hour meeting I had just endured with the church leadership—left my mind so rattled that I couldn't seem to find them.

When I finally unlocked my car door, my emotions unlocked too. I gripped the steering wheel with every ounce of strength, climbed into the driver's seat, and broke down. For a moment I just sat there, breathless, asking myself, "Is this really happening?"

My pounding heart and rapid breathing had no patience for my question. They smacked me back to reality: Leave the parking lot—now.

So I fled. My fight-or-flight response had chosen flight, and I pressed the gas as far as my black Jeep would take me. I sped away from the church, down a small road that felt like the only way to safety.

I had just been wounded—emotionally, mentally, and spiritually—by the deacons of my childhood church. I had no idea how deep the damage would run. All I knew was that I wanted to flee—to get away and never look back. I wanted to leave and never set foot in a church again. Ever.

But God knew. He knew this night would become one of the defining moments of my future. As I drove away, shaken and broken, He saw exactly what had happened. He already knew what He would do about it and what He would do in me through it.

That April evening so many years ago was the culmination of what had begun months earlier. It began when I decided to come forward to my church leadership about my abusive marriage. At first, all the deacons seemed to be in favor of helping me. But over time something in them shifted. Instead of standing with me, they decided to side with my then-husband.

Their remedy for my situation wasn't dealing with the abuse. Instead, they decided to kick me out of the church my dad had pastored, simply because I planned to file for divorce. The purpose of the meeting that night was clear: If I didn't do what they asked, they would remove me. They leveraged God for their own agenda, wanting to make an example out of a pastor's kid. They wanted to send a message, and did they ever.

One of the deacons looked me square in the face, his voice laced with disdain: "If you do this—divorce your abusive husband—God will never use you."

That single sentence—carelessly dropped from his lips—wounded me in ways I still think about. In one torrent of spiritually abusive words, he presumed to speak for a gracious God, when God can speak for Himself. He used his temporary authority to manipulate me, attempting to stop what would become a reckoning in that church.

I heard it. The whole room heard it. God heard it too.

When his words landed, the room seemed to darken. Everything else from the meeting blurred, and when it finally ended, I fled.

I drove down the avenue as fast as I possibly could. The further I was from the church, the safer I felt. It's jarring when the place meant to protect you is the one that wounds you. What do you do when a sanctuary turns savage?

A mile into my drive home, the Lord began to comfort my traumatized soul. I vividly remember His words: "I used Moses... I used Abraham... I used Peter... Do you remember? None of those men were perfect."

What the deacon board didn't know was that a year earlier I had experienced a radical conversion to Christ. As a pastor's kid, I had gone most of my life believing I was saved—yet I was one assumption away from hell. I spent that year getting to know God, and in the process, I fell in love with Jesus—the real Jesus. The Jesus I met during my conversion was nothing like the one I had assumed Him to be. As I've shared in other books, He met me in the depths of my sin and loved me forward.

I had started my relationship with the Lord that year, and it had grown into something I had always wanted but never knew was possible. I was learning how to pray and had begun depending on communicating constantly with the Lord throughout my day. As a twenty-one-year-old pastor's daughter, I had to admit that I had no idea what or who God truly was. I wasn't even sure if He was real. Yes, I knew all the stories. I could win any Bible drill you challenged me with. I knew the sixty-six books of the Bible better than the alphabet. But head knowledge doesn't get you into heaven—nor into a relationship with Jesus. As James 2:19 says, "The demons also believe, and shudder."

Yes, as a pastor's daughter, I needed to be saved. That year I finally met Jesus.

As the Holy Spirit spoke to me on the drive home, I felt a comfort I had never known before. Fleeing felt safe, but His comfort felt safer. He helped me first escape that relationship and eventually that church, even though the leadership had decided to kick me out.

I never went back to that church as a member. A few weeks later, they did follow through with church discipline in a business meeting—but by then, I had already withdrawn my membership. Just like that, I was "church homeless."

At first, being "church homeless" felt good—safe, even.

There was comfort in knowing no church could hurt me if I didn't belong to one. For a while I felt liberated. I had just walked through the most horrible situation I had ever heard of in a church, and I *never* wanted to go through anything like it again.

So church homelessness felt like the right thing to do. It felt like my only option. It seemed like the only way to protect myself from another frightening episode of "deacons gone wild," and I thought this might preserve what love I still had left for the church. At first, staying away felt liberating, but months later the loneliness began to set in.

The truth was, I didn't want to leave the church. My dad was the senior pastor, but he wasn't allowed to be involved in the process to remove me and would be terminated the following year. Some of my best memories were tied to that blacktop. My whole community was wrapped up in that place. I had babysat the children of the very deacons who now sought to excommunicate me. My roots were deep—until I had to rip them out of the soil where they had grown, only to realize they were deep only in my eyes.

The longer I stayed away, the angrier I became. The injustice kept me up at night. The betrayal made me guarded toward church leaders. The lack of compassion I had seen in those men that night caused my wound to grow even deeper.

It was in this pit—where anger began to harden into bitterness—that the Holy Spirit started to speak:

"Are you going to let these men keep you away from My house?"

"Are you going to live angry forever?"

"Are you going to let this one event keep you from everything I have for you?"

"Do you want to carry a chip on your shoulder about the church forever?"

"Did the whole church hurt you or just these few men?"

"Am I not greater than these?"

"Can I not bring justice to your situation?"

"Am I not just?"

These questions from the Lord bombarded my mind regularly. Some days they were welcome. Other days I shut them down because my anger felt good. It felt justified.

But every time the Holy Spirit challenged me, He reminded me: "I will have the final word. I will take justice into My own hands. I will fight for you. This will not stand."

As God spoke to me through His Word about His justice, I began to release my anger to Him, trusting that He would handle all that had happened. He asked me to hand over my anger, and I did—He would take it from there. My righteous anger was safe in His justice.

GOD WILL RESPOND TO THOSE WHO TREAT YOU UNJUSTLY

After all, how was I—alone—supposed to plead my case before these "leaders" who had become one voice against me? The answer was, I couldn't. They had the platform. They controlled the narrative. The entire church was under their influence—not mine. I had no voice.

It didn't matter what was right. They weren't interested in truth. They seemed far more interested in maintaining a false peace, even if it meant suppressing the truth.

But when they refused to give me a voice, God saw it. He saw the inner workings of their plans. He heard the secret conversations that took place, where they plotted against me and my family.

The Holy Spirit was present in each of those private conversations. Because He saw and heard everything, He told me to trust Him with the injustice. While they schemed against me in secret, He was already preparing His response. Folks, He had the final word. He always does. This is where I learned the following: When the enemy conspires against you in private, don't fear; the Spirit of God hears their plans.

This is hard. Trusting God with your anger is hard. Anger is a natural—and sometimes even righteous—response when you've been treated unjustly. Jesus was angry in the temple. Paul tells us in Ephesians 4:26 (NIV), "In your anger do not sin." Why? Because he knew that surrendering anger to the Lord, allowing Him to deal with injustice, is far more powerful than taking matters into your own hands. There will be times when you won't have a loud enough voice to defend yourself. For reasons beyond your control, no one will listen. Perhaps they don't believe you. Maybe they have their agenda. Either way, some things must be placed in the Lord's hands—and use faith to trust that He will take care of it in His time. That's exactly what I had to do. That's exactly what Job did.

Job's friends falsely accused him of harboring hidden sin, claiming it was the reason he was experiencing such severe trials (Job 4:3–4; Job 4:7–8; Job 8:20). But they were wrong, just as Satan is wrong when he falsely accuses us. In response Job tried desperately to defend himself, but he eventually gave up. In Job 16:2 (NIV) he calls them "miserable comforters." In Job 27:5–6 he clings to his integrity even under assault: "Far be it from me that I should declare you right; till I die I will not put away my integrity from me. I hold fast my righteousness and will not let it go; my heart does not reproach any of my days."

While Job fought hard to defend his righteousness, his words fell on deaf ears. They didn't believe him, so eventually he stopped trying to convince them. That was when God stepped in. God wasn't about to let Job's defense go unheard, because He is just. This is where the story gets good: In Job chapters 38–41 God breaks His silence, speaking first to Job and then to his friends. The justice of God couldn't remain silent while Job's righteous character was under attack. Even though God could've stayed silent and ignored Job's friends altogether, His integrity and character wouldn't allow it. He had to right the wrong of false accusations. Job's friends wouldn't listen to him, but they had no choice when it came to listening to God.

Before we look at God's words to Job's friends, let's look at several verses revealing God's heart for justice. I want you to see how seriously He takes it. God won't allow injustice against His children to stand; He takes it personally.

- **Isaiah 30:18**—"Therefore the LORD longs to be gracious to you, and therefore He waits on high to have compassion on you. For the LORD is a God of justice; how blessed are all those who long for Him."

- **Psalm 33:5**—"He [God] loves righteousness and justice; the earth is full of the lovingkindness of the LORD."

- **Psalm 37:12–15**—"The wicked plots against the righteous and gnashes at him with his teeth. The Lord laughs at him, for He sees his day is coming. The wicked have drawn the sword and bent their bow to cast down the afflicted and the needy, to slay those who are upright in conduct. Their sword will enter their own heart, and their bows will be broken."

- **Romans 12:19**—"Never take your own revenge, beloved, but leave room for the wrath of God, for it is written, 'Vengeance is Mine, I will repay,' says the Lord."

- **Proverbs 20:22**—"Do not say, 'I will repay evil'; wait for the LORD, and He will save you."

- **Deuteronomy 32:35–36**—"'Vengeance is Mine, and retribution, in due time their foot will slip; for the day of their calamity is near, and the impending things are hastening upon them.' For the LORD will vindicate His people, and will have compassion on His servants, when He sees that their strength is gone, and there is none remaining, bond or free."

- **Isaiah 42:1**—"Behold, My Servant, whom I uphold; My chosen one in whom My soul delights. I have put My spirit upon Him; He will bring forth justice to the nations."

- **Isaiah 61:8**—"For I, the LORD, love justice, I hate robbery in the burnt offering; and I will faithfully give them their recompense and make an everlasting covenant with them."

- **Luke 18:7–8** (ESV)—"And will not God give justice to his elect, who cry to him day and night? Will he delay long over them? I tell you, he will give justice to them speedily."

- **Psalm 9:7** (ESV)—"But the LORD sits enthroned forever; he has established his throne for justice."

Shall I go on? I could, but you get the point. God hates injustice. He hates that you were wronged, treated unfairly, or sinned against, and He makes it His intense mission to right that wrong. That is why we don't have to chase after justice or wear ourselves out trying to defend ourselves. God will do it for us.

Isn't it exhausting? My anger toward those who wronged me used to exhaust me. I spent countless hours of my life ruminating over something that I could never fix. It wasted energy—until I finally left those injustices with the Lord. Only then did my soul finally find peace.

Let me make a clear distinction: I am talking about *spiritual* justice. There are times when the legal system must be used—for obvious reasons, such as when crimes have been committed against us. That, too, is a way God brings justice, working through the systems in place to protect and defend the innocent. Please don't misunderstand what I am saying.

GOD'S RESPONSE TO THE INJUSTICE OF JOB

God spoke to Job, but He wasn't finished. Next, He turned His attention to Job's friends. No games, no soft introduction—just straight to the point. He addressed Eliphaz, the only friend He spoke to by name, saying,

> My wrath is kindled against you and against your two friends, because you have not spoken of Me what is right as My servant Job has. Now therefore, take for yourselves seven bulls and seven rams, and go to my servant Job, and offer up a burnt offering for yourselves, and My servant Job will pray for you. For I will accept him so that I may not do with

you according to your folly, because you have not
spoken of Me what is right, as My servant Job has.
—Job 42:7–8

You guys, they made God so mad that they had to offer
burnt offerings—and then ask Job, the guy they had spoken so
wrongly about, to pray for them. I don't know about you, but
that would've been incredibly humbling and more than a little
embarrassing. Their theology—their words about God—were
so off that God publicly called them out and made it clear
they could only be restored if Job prayed for them.

Wow, can you imagine that moment? Job, standing
there, praying on behalf of the very friends who had
wounded him so deeply? Can you imagine what he must've
felt? I'm sure he felt relief—yes—and complete vindication.
Wouldn't you?

Job's friends weren't bad men; they simply had a very limited view of who God was. Based on that limited understanding, they assumed God would side with them in their
judgment. But He didn't. God has a way of taking matters
into His precious, righteous hands and showing the whole
world who is right and who is wrong. Not only did Job witness God having his back, but we also get to see it written
in Scripture for all time: Job's friends were wrong. God's justice for Job didn't end there. Throughout His Word He continues to speak about justice—for Job and for Himself. As
we read the Book of Job, we witness God's ongoing defense
and His ongoing avenging of both His servant and His own
name against false accusations. His justice never sleeps.

God Wants to Be in Charge
of Justice for You

One of the strongest verses about God's justice on our behalf is this: "Vengeance is Mine, I will repay" (Rom. 12:19). God owns your justice—it belongs to Him. He is the warrior who steps in front of you to fix what is broken. When He says it's His problem, He means it. He wants it to be His problem. He wants to be in charge of it. God loves to exact justice on your behalf.

Why? I believe it's because He knows He can do a far better, more complete job than we ever could. He can even speak for us when we are silenced or bullied into silence. He can act with limitless resources when ours are limited. He always has access to the truth, while others can be swayed by lies. He knows exactly who has wronged us—and precisely what kind of response will set things right and repay their folly.

I realized these truths in the middle of wrestling with my anger toward the men at the church who had kicked me out. I struggled deeply when I didn't see the justice I thought should happen. I knew where I stood with God—just like Job. I knew what was right and what was wrong, but it felt as if no one else would ever know the truth, and the slander born from their decisions would linger forever.

Then God asked me a piercing question: "Am I not just?" That question began to change everything: my thinking, my prayers, even how I studied Scripture. When I came across Romans 12:19, it was like a light flipped on. That was my epiphany about justice. I realized that if justice were left in my hands, I might not deliver it strongly enough. But if I surrendered it to the Lord, His justice would be complete—enough to satisfy Him and enough to satisfy me. So

I released it. I gave it to Him. In doing so, I discovered something life-changing: God is more passionate about exacting justice on my behalf than I could ever be. He will have the final word.

LET GOD HAVE THE FINAL WORD

In 2015 I attended a conference where a man approached me and said, "Keep banging the drum of domestic violence and the church will eventually listen." His words proved prophetic. Just a year later, I was invited to commission a study with Lifeway Research, polling pastors on their churches' readiness to respond if victims of domestic violence came forward.

When the research concluded the following year, the results were sobering. Most of the churches polled weren't adequately prepared to respond to victims at the level they should be. The findings sent shock waves through the church community. Because of my personal experience—first as a victim of domestic violence and then as a survivor of spiritual abuse within my church—my story became a widely circulated narrative.

While the study did confront cover-up tactics used by some churches in cases of abuse, most saw it as a rallying cry to prepare themselves to help victims when they came forward. They accepted the challenge and began updating policies to protect victims like me. This study became a source of both freedom and hope for many.

It was just one way God brought justice for me. He allowed me to be a catalyst for educating churches worldwide on this subject—a conversation now happening regularly in the church at large. I remember the day the study was released. I could barely speak, as I was overwhelmed by the realization that I was finally experiencing the justice God promises in His Word. It was a level of justice so great that I could never have achieved it on my own. God owned my justice. This is only one example—among countless others—of the ways I've seen Him move because of what I went through. God had the final word.

Friend, where are you? Do you stay up at night replaying what happened? Have people wronged you in a season when you needed support most? Does the thought of revenge keep you awake? Does it frustrate you that God hasn't moved quickly enough to bring justice? If so, I get it. Those feelings are incredibly valid. But the truth is, God's passion is to bring justice to you. It's time to hand that zest for justice over to our able God. Surrender it fully to His care. Again, let me declare: God is passionately in love with exacting justice on your behalf, because He is passionately in love with you.

I remember the exact moment He asked me to repent of my anger and pray for those who had wronged me. I was reading this very chapter—Job 42—when the words pierced my heart and changed my life. Without hesitation I began praying by name for the church leaders who had kicked me out, telling the Lord that the justice due to me was His. I even marked the date in my Bible. In that moment it was as if a fresh wind swept through my soul, lifting the heavy burden of justice I had carried for so long. God had taken it from me. From that day forward, I was free from that anger. Just a few years later, I saw undeniable evidence of His hand at work on my behalf—through that unexpected email.

I wrote this chapter because God asked me to. I had another subject in mind, but the Lord spoke to me and made it clear that this message on justice couldn't wait. I love you, friend. I know it may be hard, but now is the time to sur-render—and watch God work.

Scan this QR code or visit AutumnMilesBooks.com/ holyghosted/resources to watch a brief video from me with encouragement and deeper insight for your journey.

Chapter 13
HOLY RESTORATION—GOD WILL RESTORE MORE THAN WHAT WAS TAKEN

We count those blessed who endured. You have heard of the endurance of Job and have seen the outcome of the Lord's dealings, that the Lord is full of compassion and is merciful.
—JAMES 5:11

I WAITED A LONG time to write this chapter. I've craved the happy ending to this hard, heavy book, chronicling our friend Job's life. I've daydreamed about how this chapter would look and how I might speak life to those places of doubt in your faith. I've lain awake in the twilight hours, asking God for wisdom to unpack His restoration power in a way that inspires you.

There isn't just one story I could tell about God's miraculous restoration. The problem isn't a lack of examples; it's that I have too many. I've sat for hours asking the Lord to reveal which story would best suit this last, most anticipated chapter—but instead of giving me just one, He reminded me of many.

Today I am overwhelmed with personal evidence of the God who restores. I feel like a seasoned attorney, ready to make my case for God's restoration before a judge and jury.

I have a storehouse overflowing with personal examples to choose from. In my Bible I keep an arsenal of time-stamped miracles—proof of His supernatural restoration—each one a compelling candidate to convince you that God's restoration is unstoppable. Yet I still can't choose just one. As eyewitnesses I've asked my children which moment best illustrates His restoration, but they couldn't pick just one. I also called my husband to ask his input—he couldn't decide either. As we recount, through tears, the tangible hand of God's restoration in our lives, the task feels impossible.

The truth is, nothing in my life was salvageable almost two and a half decades ago. Every beat of my heart, every thought in my mind, every hug from my child, every kiss from my husband, every friend I have, every dollar in my bank account, every book sold, every podcast download, every position of leadership, every theological accolade—every single thing in my life—is living proof that God restores.

My life defies the claim that evil is allowed to stand. It mocks the ideology that bad things get the final word for God's children. It rebukes a theology that doesn't leave any room for His abundant grace. I am a living illustration of what God does with the broken, the rejected, the outcast, and the misfit—because I am one.

What you see and hear from me today didn't exist until God restored it. I should be dead. I should be an addict. I should be friendless, husbandless, and childless. But God refused to let that be my story. His power stepped into my life, wrecked by sin and bad choices, and declared, "I will have the final word. I will restore her."

So I let Him. I am the product of His restoration.

Job put it this way, "The LORD has given; the LORD has taken; bless the LORD's name" (Job 1:21, CEB). In my life I've experienced times when things were stripped away without warning. But with every loss came the process—and the promise—of God's restoration.

For example, as I shared in a previous chapter, the church leadership that kicked me out told me, "God will never use you." Yet here I am, folks, more than fifteen years later, colaboring with God to lead this ministry, and among many other things, writing my fourth book—the very one you're holding in your hands right now. How does that happen? Well, God restores. In doing so, He turned the words spoken against me into lies. I know what it looked like to those men at the time. They believed their actions and words would be agreeable to the Lord, but they left the power of divine restoration out of their calculations. They overestimated their influence and underestimated God's.

I was told, "You will never marry again," after my first husband, but I met Eddie the very next month. We've been married for twenty-one years and counting. God turned those words into lies. How? God restores!

The loss of the twin girls promised during the adoption process—only later to discover we were being scammed—was devastating, as I shared in a previous chapter. We thought things couldn't get any bleaker as we processed the magnitude of that betrayal. But the restoring arm of God was already at work, declaring that loss wouldn't stand. Just a year and a half later, He gave us our double portion of blessing in Moses and Haven. The loss didn't have the final word. The restoring arm of God spoke so loudly that everyone who knew the situation heard it—and when they did, their faith grew.

Eddie and I once faced a horrible situation. A trusted adviser told us, "There is no way I can help you." Days later the entire crisis was turned on its head in our favor. How? God restores.

We lost a business, and God restored our loss.

My son battled asthma so severe it nearly took his life, and God restored his health completely.

My daughter Haven was born with a defect so severe that she suffered *death spells*, but God fully restored her.

God restores marriages.

God restores children.

God restores finances.

God restores reputations.

God restores friendships.

God restores mental health.

God restores physical health.

God restores faith with His faithfulness.

He has done every one of these for me. Loss has taught me to depend on His restoration. Over the years I've learned that when loss comes—and all seems hopeless—it's not the end of the story. I refuse to let it be. Why? Because I will stand on the restoring hand of God—a truth written in His Word and proved in my life again and again over decades.

Restoration is the end of your story, not the loss.

Loss is the middle; restoration is the end.

I won't give up in the middle, knowing God's restoration is coming. In the church, loss has been given too much power. Yes, loss is real and painful. But the faithfulness of God's restoration should have the microphone. Loss must be acknowledged and grieved, as ignoring it would reject reality. Yet, as believers in Jehovah, who raised His Son from the dead, we must train our minds to expect His restoration. Loss is not the end; restoration is.

No one truly understands what it's like to lose everything until it happens to you. Loss changes you in ways you never expect. It builds mental barriers in places you've never struggled with before. Trauma creates fears and terrifying insecurities so deep that they can haunt you if not dealt with. When everything familiar is gone—every person, every place, and every possession—the security you once found in friends, family, or even routine is stripped away. You realize those people and things were never real security. You find yourself longing for what is sure, what is unshakable.

In this life what can you count on when the "security" you trusted turns out to be fraudulent?

After my divorce, I lost everything—my friends, the only community I had ever known, pieces of my identity, and most of my possessions. I had no choice but to cling to the promise of God's restoration, because without trust in Him, I would've looked for another way to numb the pain. The loss was substantial. To me, it was everything. I had to rebuild my life from the ground up. But here's what I learned: The loss I experienced wasn't stronger than the restoring hand of God. Losing everything wasn't my end; in many ways, it was my beginning.

Radical, Unapologetic Restoration

I lost everything, as did Job. But at the height of his grief, Job proclaimed something prophetic: "As for me, I know that my Redeemer lives, and at the last He will take His stand on the earth. Even after my skin is destroyed, yet from my flesh I shall see God" (Job 19:25–26). He knew then what I learned years ago—that loss wouldn't be his final chapter. By faith he believed God would redeem what had been lost, and he was right. In Job 42:10 we see the process begin: "The Lord restored the fortunes of Job when he prayed for his friends, and the Lord increased all that

Job had twofold." In this verse the Hebrew word for *restored* is *shub* (pronounced *shoov*), a verb meaning "to turn back, return, go back, come back, repair, give back, or reverse."[1]

For some reason I think of a dog playing fetch: You throw the ball, and the dog brings it right back. It isn't a true loss; it's a temporary one. I picture the loss of all that Job held dear being so close that God simply returned it. God gave it back. While you might see that as an oversimplification of the scripture, that's how I have experienced restoration. God gives back what was lost. It really is as simple as that.

While God brought restoration, Job's prayer initiated it. The verse says, "The LORD restored the fortunes of Job when he prayed for his friends." In Matthew 5:44 (NIV), Jesus tells us, "Love your enemies and pray for those who persecute you." Job did that, and the result was the blessing and full restoration of God. Did God need Job to pray for his friends to restore? No, God could've restored everything without it. However, I believe God tested Job's heart to see whether his righteousness still stood before He brought restoration. Was Job still the same righteous man in Job 42 as in Job 1:8? A lot had happened. Had Job's heart hardened toward God because of losing everything? It could've. Did Job feel prideful when he heard God rebuke his three friends harshly, knowing he had been right about his innocence the entire time? The answer is clear—Job was the same righteous man. His heart hadn't hardened. Rather than rejecting his friends, he obeyed God and prayed for them. This pleased the heart of the Father so much so that God not only restored Job's fortunes but also brought a double portion of blessings upon Job.

Losing something or someone suddenly or tragically can cause your heart to harden. It can take you from what you once were—gracious and forgiving—to hard and cynical. I've seen losses so great do a number on some of the most righteous people's hearts. Severe loss can harden you. Severe betrayal can take your soft, pliable heart toward people and the things of God and turn it away. Being falsely accused of something, as Job was, can make you forever skeptical of people. This is no way to live, my friend. If allowed to stand, your hard heart toward people and the things of God would be a greater loss than anything else. Trust me when I say that, while a hard heart feels safer than a soft one, it robs you from the very life and restoration God desires to give you.

I completely understand that you're a survivalist who feels the need to protect yourself. It feels "wise" to put up walls— to guard yourself from ever being hurt again. I lived like that for years after I was excommunicated from my church. But I learned something sobering: Avoiding pain robbed me more than the betrayal ever did. I had hardened my heart, closing it off to certain people, and without realizing it, I had also hardened my heart toward the Lord in some ways. My inflexibility kept Him out of places He wanted to restore.

However, when I began to pray for those who hurt me, my restoration came in like a flood. That's why I am compelled to have you pause and evaluate the state of your heart. Are you cynical? Are you skeptical of people? Are you carrying a silent chip on your shoulder about God? Do you have a bad attitude about the church? Listen, I get it. But I also hear God saying, "Let that go." He wants to restore your heart and make it pliable and soft again. He wants to be your shield.

DOUBLE PORTION OF RESTORATION

I sat in a church service a few months after our adoption trauma—after being lied to by a woman who told us she was pregnant with twins when she wasn't. My heart was hard. I was angry at just about everything that had to do with adoption, ready to give it all up. Most people have no idea what an emotional roller coaster the adoption process can be unless they've lived through it. I didn't even want to attend church that day, but I've learned it's often the days when I least want to go that I often need to be there the most.

The guest speaker stood to share her testimony, and I breathed a sigh of relief, thinking I would finally have a mental break from any thoughts about adoption. But the first words out of her mouth were something like, "I've wanted to adopt since I was young." My whole body tensed. I knew God was about to speak loudly to me. She began telling us about the story of her and her husband's adoption journey, which ended in—yes, you guessed it—twin girls. Not only that, but they were also born on Christmas Eve or Christmas Day in a town named Bethlehem. (I can't remember the exact date.) Guys, I kid you not. Tears were streaming down my face, as God was speaking to my soul.

She then referenced Isaiah 61, a passage I knew well. I knew where she was going, and it was as if God was shouting in my spirit:

> Instead of your shame you will have a double portion, and instead of humiliation they will shout for joy over their portion. Therefore they will possess a double portion in their land, everlasting joy will be theirs. For, I, the LORD, love justice, I hate robbery in the burnt offering; and I will faithfully give them their recompense and make an everlasting covenant with them.
>
> —ISAIAH 61:7–8

I could barely speak, my friend. I was in a puddle. The Lord was telling me, "You will have your double portion—just wait for it. Restoration is on the way."

A year later Moses and Haven joined our family. "Instead of your shame you will have a double portion." God did exactly that. He took away our shame and restored the great loss. The loss was just the middle of the trial. Restoration was the end.

This is what God did with Job long before Isaiah's time. Job 42:10 says, "and the LORD increased all that Job had twofold." He didn't just restore; He doubled. Zechariah 9:12 also speaks of God restoring double: "This very day I am declaring that I will restore double to you." God takes restoration extremely seriously. He doesn't just restore; He overwhelmingly restores.

Before Satan attacked Job, his possessions were five thousand sheep, three thousand camels, five hundred yokes of oxen, and five hundred female donkeys (Job 1:3). When all was said and done, he ended up with fourteen thousand sheep, six thousand camels, one thousand yokes of oxen, and one thousand female donkeys (Job 42:12). God doubled it! Satan took everything Job had at the beginning, but God restored it all back and then doubled it. This, friends, is what we need to meditate on. This is who our God is. This is what He wants to do for us when we experience seasons of great loss. He is the great restorer.

I've lived this. I've experienced the promise of a double portion of blessing instead of shame. Shame isn't the end, believer—restoration is. Only a personal God, who knows exactly how much has been lost, can calculate the loss and then restore it double. Remember when I said that God was watching closely what was happening to Job? He wasn't speaking; He was silent, but He was watching. The God that knows how many hairs are on your head has counted your loss precisely and can restore to you double (Luke 12:7). He was present in Job's loss, and He was determined to restore double to him.

I wonder whether, today, you're obsessed with the loss in your life. It's easy to do. The enemy wants you to focus on the substantial losses in your health, marriage, finances, or reputation—whatever it may be—and, yes, you are free to do so. But I invite you to meditate on Job 42:10, where God restored Job in such a way that we're still reading about it today. That same God is your God. He has calculated your loss as well. We can resist believing in God's restoration and settle into bitterness—which is exactly where the enemy wants us—or we can ask for our own double portion of restoration. Let me ask you: Have you asked God to restore what has been taken? Have you boldly stood on a promise like the one in Job 42 for your own life? This truth is for you. Own it. Don't ignore it or assume it's only for someone else. Great loss can instigate a great God to greatly restore.

HOLISTIC RESTORATION

God restored Job in an overwhelming way, but He didn't stop at giving Job's stuff back. He restored his family to him, as well as what was lost socially, spiritually, financially, medically, and physically. He even restored the stolen time. God also healed the mental trauma Job endured. He isn't just interested in restoring one piece of what was taken. He wants to overwhelmingly, holistically restore *all* that you've lost. Job never asked for his stuff back. He never even asked for his children back. All Job wanted was for the voice of God to be restored to him. It reminds me of the promise in Matthew 6:33, "Seek first His kingdom and His righteousness, and all these things will be added to you." The Book of Job is a living illustration of that truth.

Job 42:11 says that when the trials ended, Job's siblings came and "ate bread with him in his house; and they sympathized with him." A short time before, Job was considered an outcast. Yet now, as part of his holistic restoration, his siblings were back in his home, and social restoration started. They "consoled him," and emotional restoration followed. They didn't leave without giving him "one piece of money," marking the start of financial restoration. (Fun aside: The reference to a "piece of money" is one reason scholars date the Book of Job as potentially the oldest book in the Bible. Since it's thought to be pre-Mosaic, this terminology fits. Later, it would have been called a shekel.) OK, back to restoration. They also gave Job a "gold ring," possibly for the nose or ear, symbolizing that the honor and respect of his siblings had been restored. Once estranged from them, Job's relationship was mended, and the process of holistic restoration had begun—though it would still unfold over time.

THE PROCESS OF RESTORATION

Let's talk about the *process* of restoration. Most of us are impatient. We want God to restore everything we've lost instantly. And if we are honest, when He doesn't, we feel a certain kind of way about it. Let me ask you this question: Does it truly matter how long restoration takes if we know God will restore? While He can restore everything in an instant, He usually doesn't. He didn't restore everything to Job instantly—there was a process. It takes time for livestock to be born, for wealth to grow, and for word to spread through a community that God vindicated you. Sometimes it even takes time for health to return.

If you're skeptical that God will restore what you've lost, let me ask you this: Have you taken a moment to evaluate your life to see whether the process has already begun? If it has, it will continue to mature. Sometimes you hardly notice that His restoration has been quietly unfolding for years. God didn't restore Job all at once; He restored him little by little until the task was complete. For example, God began to restore Job's children one at a time. The children he lost couldn't be replaced, and the text doesn't suggest the new children were a replacement but rather a restoration of what was taken. The conception and birth of each of those ten children took time. When Job's family was complete again, he had the joy of seeing four generations of children and grandchildren (Job 42:16).

Your restoration will be a process. It won't happen all at once. Be patient with God's timing and pay attention—it may have already begun. Take a minute to evaluate the area of loss in your life: Do you see healing? Do you see growth? Do you see increase? However small, praise God for the beginning of His restoration. He is *more* than able to do immeasurably more than we can ask or imagine (Eph. 3:20).

SATAN CAN'T TAKE MORE THAN GOD CAN RESTORE

"But in all these things we overwhelmingly conquer through Him who loved us" (Rom. 8:37). Satan will never outdo God. No competition exists—God wins in an overwhelming fashion every time. The threat of the enemy is fraudulent to those who call God their King. Eddie and I went through a season of great loss a few years back during COVID-19. Loss seemed to surround us on all sides. From financial, professional, and communal losses, I was dazed, confused, and even in a state of shock. Daily losses dictated where my mind rested. Loss dominated my thoughts, while restoration wasn't even a thought. While we were reeling, like the rest of the world, the Lord spoke to my Spirit and said, "Satan cannot take more than I can restore." My mind went immediately back to one of my favorite passages, Joel 2:25 (NIV): "I will repay you for the years the locusts have eaten." That truth became my mantra in 2020. Satan may have taken it, but God will restore it. I found my mind resting on that promise rather than all the loss. While the loss screamed at me, the promise of restoration comforted me. In the past few years, we've seen great increase in every area of loss. God has restored—or has begun the restoration process—in every bleak area of deficit. Satan couldn't take more than God could restore, even when he tried his hardest.

SATAN HAS TO WATCH THE RESTORATION PROCESS

While the enemy oversaw the destruction process in Job's life, he had to watch God put it all back together. He had to watch God undo everything he tried to do. Piece by piece he saw that his power was limited, and God's power was supreme over his destruction. God reversed the enemy's destruction. Little by little he saw that his agenda didn't work, couldn't work, and was never going to work. Satan couldn't stop the God who stopped him. He wasn't strong enough. So he had to stand by while Job was being given a double portion and had to watch it all unfold. The mark of true defeat is to watch what was claimed as a victory by the enemy be overcome by the goodness of God. This proves that nothing Satan does is permanent. In the end it will all be overcome. Restoration comes to even the greatest, most devastating loss. The loss isn't the end; restoration is. Ultimately, the only thing God needs to restore is Himself.

THE ONE THING THAT DIDN'T NEED TO BE RESTORED

The only thing that didn't need to be restored in the entire Book of Job was his faith. Satan was after it. He threw everything at Job, but Job's faith was never taken from him, because his faith was never in Satan's power—it was in God's alone. Satan wasn't after Job's stuff; he was after his faith. True victory for the enemy would've been a surrender of Job's faith, and that was never on the table.

Satan overshot his shot with Job. He miscalculated. He assumed Job's faith was a product of blessing, but he didn't know it had the foundation of the bedrock of Yahweh. Job's life plays like a living example to the words of Jesus:

> Therefore everyone who hears these words of Mine and acts on them, may be compared to a wise man who built his house on the rock. And the rain fell, and the floods came, and the winds blew and slammed against that house; and yet it did not fall, for it had been founded on the rock.
> —MATTHEW 7:24–25

Even the fiercest storm wasn't strong enough to shake the faith of a wise man who knew it all could be rebuilt by the rock.

God offered Job because He knew Job's faith was stronger than Satan's arrow. Satan was never going to get access to Job's faith, so he fought a losing battle from the start. Silence from God didn't shake Job's faith. Losing everything didn't shake Job's faith. Being betrayed by his friends didn't shake

Job's faith. Why? Because none of those things are as durable as the faith connection to our God. It's indestructible. The only way to destroy it is to give it away.

Your faith is that powerful too. Satan isn't after your stuff, health, marriage, or reputation—he is after your faith. Cling to it, fellow soldier. It is the most valuable thing that you possess. Nothing is stronger.

> And I heard a loud voice saying in heaven, now is come salvation, and strength, and the kingdom of our God, and the power of his Christ: for the accuser of our brethren is cast down, which accused them before God day and night. And they overcame him by the blood of the Lamb, and by the word of their testimony; and they loved not their lives unto the death.
>
> —REVELATION 12:10–11, KJV

Scan this QR code or visit AutumnMilesBooks.com/holyghosted/resources to watch a brief video from me with encouragement and deeper insight for your journey.

A PERSONAL INVITATION
FROM THE AUTHOR

GOD LOVES YOU deeply. His Word is filled with promises that reveal His desire to bring healing, hope, and abundant life to every area of your being—body, mind, and spirit. More than anything, He wants a personal relationship with you through His Son, Jesus Christ.

If you've never invited Jesus into your life, you can do so right now. It's not about religion—it's about a relationship with the One who knows you completely and loves you unconditionally. If you're ready to take that step, simply pray this prayer with a sincere heart:

> *Lord Jesus, I want to know You as my Savior and Lord. I confess and believe that You are the Son of God and that You died for my sins. I believe You rose from the dead and are alive today. Please forgive me for my sins. I invite You into my heart and my life. Make me new. Help me walk with You, grow in Your love, and live for You every day. In Jesus' name, amen.*

If you just prayed that prayer, you've made the most important decision of your life. All heaven rejoices with you, as do I! You are now a child of God, and your journey with Him has just begun. Please contact my publisher at pray4me@charismamedia.com if you accepted Jesus today or if this book has encouraged or impacted your life in any way. We'd love to celebrate with you and send you free materials to help strengthen your faith. We look forward to hearing from you.

NOTES

CHAPTER 1

1. Katharine J. Dell, Suzanna R. Millar, and Arthur Keefer, eds., *The Cambridge Companion to Biblical Wisdom Literature* (Cambridge University Press, 2020), 70–84, https://doi.org/10.1017/9781108673082.
2. Blue Letter Bible, "*'îyôb*," accessed August 1, 2025, https://www.blueletterbible.org/lexicon/h347/niv/wlc/0-1/.

CHAPTER 2

1. A. W. Tozer, *The Pursuit of God* (Christian Publications, 1982), 20–24.

CHAPTER 4

1. Shaun McAfee, "Is Job Truly the Oldest Book in the Bible?," *Catholic Exchange*, February 12, 2025, https://catholicexchange.com/is-job-truly-the-oldest-book-in-the-bible/.
2. Bible Hub, "Genesis 18:12," accessed August 1, 2025, https://biblehub.com/lexicon/genesis/18-12.htm.

CHAPTER 6

1. Kim Toscano, "14 Hedge Plants That Will Add Privacy and Beauty To Your Garden," *Southern Living*, April 25, 2025, https://www.southernliving.com/hedge-plants-for-privacy-11722195.
2. Toscano, "14 Hedge Plants That Will Add Privacy."
3. The Investopedia Team, "Hedge: Definition and How It Works in Investing," Investopedia, accessed

August 1, 2025, https://www.investopedia.com/
terms/h/hedge.asp.

4. Blue Letter Bible, "*šûk̠*," accessed September 19,
   2025, https://www.blueletterbible.org/lexicon/h7753/
   nasb20/wlc/0-1/.
5. Blue Letter Bible, "*šûk̠*."
6. Blue Letter Bible, "*šûk̠*."

CHAPTER 9

1. *Merriam-Webster*, "Theodicy," accessed August 1,
   2025, https://www.merriam-webster.com/dictionary/
   theodicy.
2. *Merriam-Webster*, "Theology," accessed August 1,
   2025, https://www.merriam-webster.com/dictionary/
   theology.
3. Bible Hub, "3068. Yhvh," accessed August 9, 2025,
   https://biblehub.com/hebrew/3068.htm.
4. *Encyclopaedia Britannica*, "Yahweh," accessed August
   1, 2025, https://www.britannica.com/topic/Yahweh.
5. Bible Hub, "5591. ca'ar," accessed August 1, 2025,
   https://biblehub.com/hebrew/5591.htm.
6. *Encyclopaedia Britannica*, "Behemoth," accessed
   August 1, 2025, https://www.britannica.com/topic/
   Behemoth.
7. Ps. 74:14; Isa. 27:1.

CHAPTER 11

1. Bible Hub, "5162. nacham," accessed August 1, 2025,
   https://www.biblehub.com/hebrew/5162.htm.

CHAPTER 13

1. Bible Hub, "7725. shub," accessed August 1, 2025.
   https://biblehub.com/hebrew/7725.htm.

ABOUT THE AUTHOR

Autumn is the founder and CEO of *Autumn Miles Ministries*, an organization devoted to spiritually challenging the way people think. Autumn's passion is to see people everywhere transformed by God's Word. She started her own ministry in 2010 and has taught and led others to become more passionate about Jesus through hosting over twenty-five conferences, creating online resources, leading a small group ministry, and developing leadership programs. For eighteen years, she has also taught leadership development to women's ministry students at Liberty University.

Autumn is the host of *The Autumn Miles Show,* a podcast striving to present its audience with bold truth coupled with raw faith. Before she started her podcast, Autumn hosted her own daily radio show on Salem Radio in Dallas/Fort Worth.

Autumn has authored a total of four books: *Appointed* (Baker Publishing, 2014); *I Am Rahab* (Worthy Publishing, 2018); *Gangster Prayer* (Worthy Publishing, 2019); and now *Holy Ghosted* (Charisma Publishing, 2026).

Along with writing books, she has also written for many prestigious news and media outlets, including *Christianity Today,* Fox News, *The Washington Post,* and Religion News Service. She was also a regular writer for *The Blaze.*

As a survivor, Autumn is a passionate advocate for domestic violence victims. In 2016 she partnered with Lifeway Research to commission a study on domestic violence and the church. This study helps equip churches across the country with the education and awareness that they need to plan to minister to a victim of domestic violence.

Autumn travels, speaks at conferences and events, teaches and preaches the Bible, and regularly appears on various media outlets.

She is passionate about women in ministry, Biblical literacy, leadership development, and adoption.

Her larger-than-life yet down-to-earth personality and her tenacious, driven leadership style have enabled her to live out her life mission: to infect and affect all she meets with the passion of Jesus Christ.

She has been married since 2004 to Eddie Miles, and they have four beautiful children: Grace, Jude, Moses, and Haven.